FINAL COMMAND

ACTION MANUAL

FINAL COMMAND

ACTION MANUAL

CLAUDE KING

FINAL COMMAND RESOURCES™
Murfreesboro, Tennessee

ISBN 0-9651288-1-4

Published by
Final Command Resources™
P. O. Box 332503
Murfreesboro, TN 37133-2503

For information regarding language translations, overseas publication
rights, or customized editions contact the publisher at the address
above or by e-mail at: info@FinalCommand.com. Please note that we
do not accept unsolicited manuscripts.

1 2 3 4 5 6 7 8 9 10 — 05 04 03 02 01

Printed in the USA

Order additional copies from www.FinalCommand.com

CONTENTS

Actions to Help You Obey the Final Command

SEVEN STAGES FOR MAKING DISCIPLES

Back in the early 1980's, I came across a book that was filled with very practical ways to help Christians introduce people to Jesus Christ through their relationships. In 1999 I had the privilege of revising that book in order to introduce its message to a new generation. Basically I reorganized the content around seven stages for making disciples. Once the book was released, I introduced those seven stages to some discipleship groups and to my church. I saw people immediately begin to connect with practical steps they could take to obey the Lord's command to make disciples.

Seeing the activity of God around me, I began to ask the Lord how I was to join Him in what he was doing. *Final Command* is part of the message God began to speak to my own heart. It is my offering to help you (and me) experience the joy of being laborers together with God in the redemption of a lost world.

Because I personally have been so deeply impacted by Oscar Thompson's *Concentric Circles of Concern*, I want to introduce you to his message by overviewing the seven stages for making disciples. Though this *Final Command* study can stand alone, I would encourage you to get a copy of *Concentric Circles of Concern: Seven Stages for Making Disciples*. It gives a thorough explanation of seven stages for making disciples and, more importantly, includes some very inspiring illustrations to guide and encourage you to make disciples of those in your circles of influence. I am moved every time I read Oscar's stories, and they increase my faith to believe God to work in my relationships and in my church, too.

Before we move to obeying the final command, let's look quickly at seven stages for making disciples. You need to know that every believer and every church can participate in the process of making disciples. Not every one will be equally gifted in the different actions described below. But by working together as the Body of Christ, we can indeed make disciples of the nations. The diagram below is a circular "map" of those seven stages for making disciples.

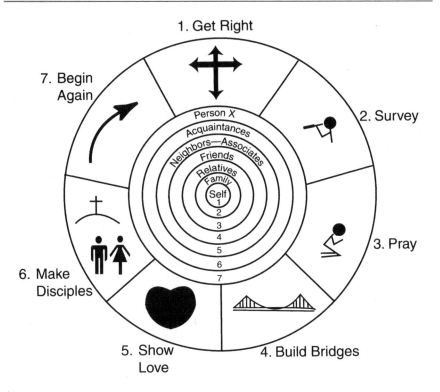

Stage 1: Get Right—Get right with God, self, and others.
Stage 2: Survey—Survey your relationships.
Stage 3: Pray—Work with God through prayer.
Stage 4: Build Bridges—Build relationship bridges to people.
Stage 5: Show Love—Show God's love by meeting needs.
Stage 6: Make Disciples—Make disciples and help them grow.
Stage 7: Begin Again—Help new Christians make disciples.

Stage 1: Get Right. The beginning place for everything is a right relationship with God. First you must come to God on His conditions for forgiveness and salvation. You also must be in right fellowship with God by remaining clean from sin and obedient to Him. In this right relationship with Him, His Spirit can flow through your life to point others to Christ.

Once you have a right vertical relationship with your heavenly Father, God moves you to correct relationships with others. You cannot be right with God and still have broken relationships with others. Reconciled relationships with others will clean the channel in your life so that the love of God can flow through you to others around you. The gospel will move through these right relationships.

Stage 2: Survey. When people begin to identify the people in their Concentric Circles of influence, they find all kinds of people who need the Lord. This survey becomes a prayer list for you to begin praying for those God has brought into your Concentric Circles.

Stage 3: Pray. When you pray, you enter the throne room of heaven where the decisions are made that govern the universe. God invites us to pray so that when He answers we will know He did it. He will get glory to Himself. As you pray for the people in your survey, you will watch to see where God is working in their lives. When you become aware of needs that will be your invitation to join God and show His love to the needy person. God will do some things in answer to believing prayer that will be accomplished in no other way.

Stage 4: Build Bridges. Sometimes your relationship with people in your Concentric Circles is so shallow or distant you have little way of reaching out to the person in love. At other times you will become aware of a person who needs the Lord and you intentionally will begin building a relationship bridge to that person so that God's love can flow to him or her.

Stage 5: Show Love. One of the best ways to be used by God in reaching your world is by showing God's love. Love is meeting needs. As God engineers circumstances in the lives of those you are praying for, He will create an opportunity for the person to experience His love through your life. As He loves the person through you by meeting his or her needs, He will begin drawing that person to His Son.

Stage 6: Make Disciples. Eventually you will reach a point where you need to confront a person with the claims of Jesus Christ on his or her life. When you see other people as God sees them—helplessly lost without Christ, you will want to share with them the good news you know about Christ. You will point them to God and His conditions for salvation.

Your responsibility is to bear witness of the Christ who lives in you. You tell about your faith in Him. The Holy Spirit is the one with the responsibility of bringing conviction of sin. He is the One who will convince the person of the truth of the gospel. When a person yields his or her life to Christ, you will be able to rejoice with the angles in heaven. You will experience the joy of being used by God to see a miracle happen in changing a life. After people turn to Christ, they need to grow as disciples of Christ.

Stage 7: Begin Again. Making disciples does not end with a decision to follow Christ. That is the beginning. Helping a new Christian grow into a fully devoted follower of Jesus Christ is also a part of the church's assignment in making disciples. You will be able to help others get right with God, self, and others. You will help them survey, pray, and build bridges to the people in their Concentric Circles of Concern. You can encourage them as they become channels of God's love. Then you will be able to rejoice with them when they see their loved ones, friends, and associates become disciples of Jesus Christ.

CONCENTRIC CIRCLES OF CONCERN
Seven Stages for Making Disciples
By W. Oscar Thompson, Jr., Carolyn Thompson Ritzmann, and Claude V. King. Broadman & Holman Publishers, 1999. (ISBN 080541959-4) Available from:
• your local Christian bookstore
• one of the Internet bookstore services
• LifeWay Christian Bookstores 1-800-448-8032

How Is *Final Command Action Manual* Different?

You might ask, How is *Final Command* different? Proverbs 16:3 reads, "Commit thy works unto the Lord, and thy thoughts shall be established" (KJV). We normally take just the opposite approach to a task. We try to understand the mental aspects of a project and gain the personal motivation first; then we begin to take action. In a sense *Concentric Circles of Concern* takes this approach. It helps you understand some very practical how-tos and seeks to motivate you to obey. That is a very valid approach and tens of thousands have been deeply blessed by Oscar Thompson's message.

In *Final Command Action Manual* I'll follow the Proverbs 16:3 order more directly. I will ask you to start obeying the final command of the Lord by doing things that are likely to bear fruit and contribute to the task. As you commit your works to the Lord, you will begin to experience God working in and through you. Then, God will bring about the changes in your thinking and motivation to be an active participant in His work of world redemption. In other words, choose to obey Him and He will take care of the rest!

INTRODUCTIONS

USING FINAL COMMAND ACTION MANUAL

In the following pages you will be reminded of the final command Jesus gave to His followers: "As you are going, make disciples of all the nations." Jesus also told us, "Lift up your eyes and look at the fields, for they are already white for harvest!" (John 4:35). This book has been designed to help you and your church work together to bring in the harvest where you are and everywhere God calls you... even to the ends of the earth.

This book will guide you to work through the process of making disciples. For best results, work through it with other believers in a small group within the church—whether that is a Sunday School class, a cell group, or some other small group. We all are commanded to make disciples, but we also are gifted in different ways. Some will be more gifted than others at different stages in the process. Others in the Body of Christ will be gifted in the areas where your gifts are not as strong. By working together, we can and must obey the final command together!

Pray

When Jesus said the harvest is great and ripe, He said, "pray the Lord of the harvest to send out laborers into His harvest" (Luke 10:2). The harvest is God's work. He has taken the initiative to invite our involvement first in prayer. As you consider using *Final Command*, pray that the Lord of the harvest will call forth laborers from your church to bring in the harvest where you are. Ask the Lord to guide you in deciding when, how, and with whom you will use *Final Command*. When you pray, be prepared to answer "yes" to God's assignment for you.

Spiritual Preparation

When Jesus gave the final command in Luke's gospel, He said, "'Stay in the city until you have been clothed with power from on high'" (Luke 24:49). The disciples needed the fulness and power of the Holy Spirit to be faithful and fruitful witnesses of Jesus Christ. You, too, need to be "clothed with power from on high." Spend time individually and as a church seeking to be clean, pure, and holy vessels that God can fill and use. I've prepared *Come to the Lord's Table: A Sacred Assembly for the Church* (see details on page 109) as a tool that will guide you in a time of consecrating yourselves to the Lord. You may want to use it or a similar process prior to using *Final Command*. Ask the Holy Spirit to guide you.

Decide on a Use Plan

This action manual has several possible uses. Choose the one that will be most helpful to your church or small group. Small Group Study Suggestions start on page 100.

1. Final Command Workshop. Use *Final Command* as a workshop manual. Plan a workshop of about four or five hours on a Friday night, a Saturday, a Sunday afternoon or evening, or on two consecutive weeknights. Leaders can use illustrations from *Concentric Circles of Concern* and/or their own experiences to guide participants to understand and start applying the seven actions in the Final Command process. Be prepared to summarize content and then guide participants to survey their world, identify their most wanted, pray, reconcile relationships, introduce Jesus Christ, etc. Focus on taking action during the workshop. Check our web site for workshop helps: www.FinalCommand.com

2. Special Short-Term Study. Distribute *Final Command Action Manuals* and make assignments before the first session. Take your time helping each other understand and begin participating in the process of making disciples.

3. Churchwide Emphasis. Your pastor or a church staff person can follow the short-term study approach in a churchwide or large group setting (e.g. Sunday or Wednesday nights).

4. Supplement for Your Small Group's Ongoing Study. Distribute a copy of *Final Command* to each member of your Sunday School class or other small group. Give brief assignments each week. Encourage participants to begin surveying their world and praying for those on their surveys. Use a few minutes before starting your regular study each week to review what you are learning from *Final Command*. Discuss ideas you have for applying the truths, hear testimonies, and take time to pray in groups of three or four. Watch for opportunities to invite your "most wanted" to join your small group Bible study.

5. Retreat. Introduce *Final Command* during a retreat and guide participants to begin surveying the relationships in their world, praying together, and discussing their strategies for culti-

vating relationships, revealing God's mercy and love, and introducing Jesus Christ to others.

6. Individual Study. You can use *Final Command* on your
own, if you choose. Doing so, however, will limit your access to
the complementary gifts, prayers, and encouragement from the
rest of the Body of Christ. You still can be obedient to the final
command whether the rest of your church is ready or not.

7. Citywide Simultaneous Approach. Christians from a variety of denominations and traditions are beginning to work together more intentionally to reach their city for Christ. Churches
could bind together in a simultaneous study of *Come to the Lord's
Table* and celebrate the Lord's Supper or Communion in individual churches as spiritual preparation for reaching their city. Then
Final Command workshops can be conducted in a variety of
times or settings. By the time most of the Christians in a city have
compiled their surveys of their world, many, if not most, of the
people in the city would be on someone's prayer list. A joint con-
cert of prayer for the city could provide the opportunity to enter
into the Final Command Covenant (pp. 106-108) with one another. People with common interests could be networked together to
reach people groups within the city. Pray and consider what the
Lord might have you do in your city.

Learning Activities

This book may be a little different than most books you've read.
I'd like to help you obey the final command and not just learn
about it. In order to do this I will give you learning activities or
assignments to help you obey the Lord's final command. Jesus
condemned the Jewish leaders for laying heavy burdens upon
the people through their laws without doing anything to help
the people obey. I've compiled this book to help you <u>obey</u> the
final command—it shouldn't be a burden too heavy to carry.
Respond to every learning activity and help others around you
do the same. *Together* we can obey the final command!

Optional Reading from *Concentric Circles of Concern*

Throughout this manual, I will make suggestions for optional
reading assignments from *Concentric Circles of Concern*. These
will include inspiring stories and illustrations related to the
action being discussed. These readings are not essential, but
they greatly will enrich your experience and understanding.

HELPING YOU OBEY THE FINAL COMMAND

In the pages that follow I want to help you, your small group, and your church obey the final command. I've developed the following diagram to illustrate the process.

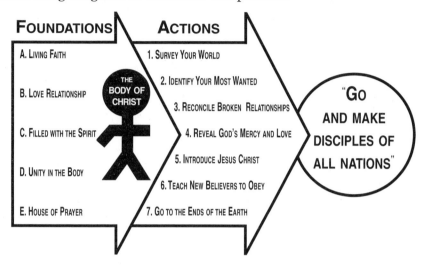

Perhaps some of you have studied *Experiencing God* or *Fresh Encounter* that I coauthored with Henry Blackaby (see p. 111 for descriptions if you haven't). The diagrams for both those courses include an arrow across the top indicating the truth that God is working in His world to accomplish His Kingdom purposes. God's ultimate objective in all His work is to reconcile a lost world to Himself through His Son Jesus Christ. He has chosen, however, to involve us in His work—both as individuals and as the Body of Christ. When we are rightly related to God, He works through us to accomplish His purposes of reconciliation in the lost world.

In the diagram for *Final Command* you will notice a similarity to the diagrams from the two other courses. When the Body of Christ is rightly related to God, we can work together with God to obey His final command and see Him accomplish His work by bringing lost people to faith in His Son. When God does this quickly and in large numbers or high percentages, we call the result a spiritual awakening. That is God's will for your world. But the winning of a lost world is dependent upon the church being clean and useable for the work. It is also dependent upon the church's obedience to the command of the Lord to make disciples as we go about our work in the world. This action manual focuses attention on the second half of the arrow. Use of *Come to the Lord's Table* should help with many of the foundation areas so that you will be spiritually prepared to obey the final command.

Foundations

The foundations describe qualities or conditions that are essential for a healthy and fruitful Body of Christ. These are areas in your personal and church life that may need renewal in order to be fruitful in obedience to the final command. If you realize your church is weak in one of these foundation areas, you will want to give special attention to it. These foundations include:

A. Living Faith. One of the great needs of many churches is to help their members come into a living faith relationship with Jesus Christ. Too many people have joined a church without ever experiencing a life changing relationship with Jesus Christ in conversion. Without a converted church membership, a church cannot be a functioning *Body of Christ*. Mere men and women have no genuine life in Christ that they can tell others about. Without a living faith, a church is merely an organization without power and without a story to tell.

B. Love Relationship. The first and greatest command is that we are to love the Lord our God with our total being. Jesus said that when we love Him we will obey His commands. When sin gets in the way of a right love relationship with God, members of the Body do not obey Christ's commands. They don't have a clear conscience; and, therefore, avoid witnessing to others because of their hypocrisy. Apart from a right love relationship, members will not possess a love like God's for a lost world. They will not care that people die and enter a godless eternity. A healthy and functioning Body of Christ will make Christ their *first love*. They will share His love for a lost world, and they will obey His commands—including the final command.

C. Filled with the Spirit. Apart from God, we can do nothing. Only when God is present in us by His Holy Spirit will He be able to work through us to accomplish His purposes. Jesus told His first disciples to wait in Jerusalem until they had been filled with the Holy Spirit. Then they would have all the power needed to be faithful and fruitful witnesses of His to the world. The Body of Christ today also must be filled with His Spirit. Our great need is to empty ourselves of self, sin, and the world so that the Holy Spirit has an empty vessel to fill. A Holy Spirit filled Body of Christ has all the power of God available to carry the gospel to a lost world.

D. Unity in the Body. Just before He went to the cross, Jesus prayed three times that God would bring His disciples to oneness and unity so that the world would know that He was sent from God. When God takes a group of people who have many and great differences and makes them one in Christ, He displays a power and greatness that the world cannot reproduce. Strife and conflict are the norms in the world. Our unity is what will convince a lost world that Christ our Savior is indeed the Son of God and Savior of the World. The reverse, however, is also true. Our lack of unity is the greatest hindrance to convincing people that Jesus is God's Son.

E. House of Prayer. The prayer life of your church is not just a religious activity you go through. It is your vital connection to the God of the universe who guides and directs your lives in keeping with His eternal purposes. Maintaining a close communion with God will keep you aware of His holiness and help you see your own sinfulness leading you to repentance. In a house of prayer, God's people find continual cleansing and renewal. They share God's heartbeat for the lost world. In this intimate communion with the Lord, volunteers readily respond to God's calling to the harvest. They receive His directions for their work. God's presence and power are manifested in and through a house of prayer. When, however, a church fails to be a house of prayer, the members are on their way to becoming a den of robbers and thieves (Jer. 7:9-11; Luke 19:46). In a "den of thieves" people live in sin just like the rest of the world and think they have God's approval, acceptance, and protection. We must become a house of prayer to be most fruitful for the Kingdom.

In one sense these foundations are prerequisites for fruitful obedience to the final command. To the degree that your church falls short of God's ideal in these areas, you will be limited in the responsiveness and fruitfulness of your efforts to reach the lost for faith in Christ. This action manual is not designed to develop strengths in these areas. Remember, however, you need not wait for perfection in these areas to begin obedience to the final command. Obedience in one area always strengthens you for obedience in other areas.

Actions

[Note: My listing of the following actions has been influenced by my work with Oscar Thompson's *Concentric Circles of Concern*. I commend his message to you for inspiration and insight in obeying the final command.]

Once you have begun to establish strong foundations in your church's walk with God, the seven actions in the second half of the arrow can help you in your obedience to the final command.

Though we must continually work on right foundations, I believe we must go on to obedience. In this action manual, I will guide you to take these seven actions as a step of obedience to the final command. You will very quickly realize that you are absolutely dependent on God for everything you are doing. You will realize how clean and right you must be in order to see change in the lives of others. As you obey the final command, you will seek the Lord's help in right foundations. The stronger the foundations, the more fruitful and joyful will be the experiences in these actions. These two parts of the final command process will work in a cycle to draw you and your church ever closer to being the healthy and functioning Body of Christ God intends for you to be.

In this action manual, you will work with other members of your church to do your part in obeying the final command. Together with others you will...

1. Survey Your World. Everyone has relationships with people in their circles of influence. You will begin making a list of people in your world. This list becomes your prayer list through which God may point you to people He is preparing to draw to Himself through you.

2. Identify Your Most Wanted. Jesus' approach to doing the will of His Father was to look to see where the Father was working and join Him (John 5:17-20). I will help you watch the people in your relationships to identify those with whom God may already be working. As God begins to reveal these to you, you will gather helpful information about each one. I'll give you some very specific ways to pray for these most wanted people as you watch for opportunities to join God working in their lives.

3. Reconcile Broken Relationships. Broken relationships can hinder your willingness to be a witness to a person or group. These must be reconciled not only for you to be right with God, but also as a means of preparing a clear channel through which the gospel about Jesus Christ can flow.

4. Reveal God's Mercy and Love. You are probably never more like Jesus than when you choose to forgive and when you demonstrate Godlike love toward others. You will begin to watch and pray for opportunities to reveal God to those around you and especially to your most wanted. Where relationships are shallow, you will begin building relationship bridges over which God's love can travel.

5. Introduce Jesus Christ. Ministry and prayer alone will not bring a person to faith in Jesus Christ. A person must hear the gospel about Jesus Christ and make a choice to die to self and live to Christ. You will identify very practical ways you can introduce others to Jesus Christ. You also will understand ways members of the Body of Christ can work together with you to see people introduced to the Savior. Together with the Body of Christ, you will begin introducing people to your Savior.

6. Teach New Believers to Obey. Part of the final command of the Lord is to teach disciples to obey everything He has commanded them. You will work together with the Body to teach obedience to others in the Body. You will help new believers to begin obedience to the final command.

7. Go to the Ends of the Earth. The final command extends to the ends of the earth. You will identify ways you can participate in taking the gospel to the ends of the earth first hand and through supporting others who go.

JESUS' FINAL COMMAND

Final words of famous people are long remembered and often quoted. When a person knows he is on his death bed, he might even prepare a final statement of challenge to family and friends. Final words can have great significance for the next generation.

Jesus Christ came to provide salvation for all mankind. Following His death, burial, and resurrection, Jesus spent forty days giving His disciples their final instructions to guide the church until His second coming. Not many of those words were recorded in the Scripture for us to read. But some were recorded, and they were perhaps his most important *last words*.

Just before Jesus ascended into heaven, He gave *one final command* to His disciples. He didn't want His disciples to miss this most important commission for the church. Actually each of the Gospel writers records a variation of the command indicating that Jesus gave special attention to it during His final days on earth. Matthew gives us probably the most well-known statement of the final command of our Lord. Jesus said:

> "All authority in heaven and on earth has been given to me. Therefore go and make disciples of all nations, baptizing them in the name of the Father and of the Son and of the Holy Spirit, and teaching them to obey everything I have commanded you. And surely I am with you always, to the very end of the age" (Matt. 28:18-20).

Mark's Gospel records Jesus saying to them, "Go into all the world and preach the good news to all creation" (Mark 16:15).

In Luke Jesus said, "This is what is written: The Christ will suffer and rise from the dead on the third day, and repentance and forgiveness of sins will be preached in his name to all nations, beginning at Jerusalem. You are witnesses of these things" (Luke 24:46-48).

And John records Jesus saying, "As the Father has sent Me, I am sending you" (John 20:21).

This final command sometimes is called the Great Commission. In commissioning His disciples Jesus gave this one great and final assignment to the church:

Go and make disciples of all nations.

In giving this assignment, Jesus reminded His followers that ALL the authority of the universe belonged to Him. Jesus Christ has the exclusive right to command us to make disciples of all peoples. But He also possesses ALL the power of the universe to enable us to carry out the final command. He asks of us only what He also will empower us to do!

He does not expect us to labor alone, either. He promised to be with us always. He promises us the power and presence of the Holy Spirit to be His witnesses:

> "You will receive power when the Holy Spirit comes on you; and you will be my witnesses in Jerusalem, and in all Judea and Samaria, and to the ends of the earth" (Acts 1:8).

His final command to the church was and still is that we are to be His witnesses and make disciples of all peoples of the earth. Jesus gave this assignment to all His disciples. Every born again believer has a part to play in obedience to the final command of our Lord.

Delayed Spiritual Awakening?

For years many Christians have been seeking God for revival among His people in our land. We've been seeking a spiritual awakening of the lost to faith in Christ. God made a promise regarding the healing of a nation:

> "If My people who are called by My name will humble themselves, and pray and seek My face, and turn from their wicked ways, then I will hear from heaven, and will forgive their sin and heal their land" (2 Chron. 7:14).

Much has been done to humble ourselves. Many are praying and seeking God's face like never before in the history of the world. Much is being done to confess and seek forgiveness for our sin and return to the Lord in obedience. Yet, God has not yet seen fit to pour out a nationwide spiritual awakening in keeping with His promise. Lost people are not coming to faith in Christ in massive numbers as we would expect in a spiritual awakening. I've been asking the Lord, Why? Lord, what is still lacking for You to heal our land?

Only God fully knows the answer to that question. Surely, we have much for which we still must repent. However, I'm convinced that one of the remaining areas of required repentance is _obedience to the final command_. A very high percentage of God's people are practicing disobedience to this one command. How can we expect a spiritual awakening in our land when the great and final command of our Lord goes undone and is regularly and massively disobeyed by His people?

Would you say that your church as a whole is obeying the final command in a way that pleases and honors God? Are you personally obeying the final command?

➡ **Which of the following best describes your <u>personal</u> obedience to the final command? Check one.**

     ❏ a. I plead ignorance. I didn't know about this command (or I assumed it was an assignment for someone else). I haven't obeyed it.

     ❏ b. I've known about the command, but most of the time I haven't known what to say or do. I haven't obeyed.

     ❏ c. I've made some attempts at being a witness for the Lord, but I confess that I haven't taken this command as seriously as I know the Lord desires.

     ❏ d. I am seeking through my life and words to obey the final command depending on the Holy Spirit to empower me.

Most of us and most of our churches would have to confess that we are living in disobedience to the final command. I can't speak for you, but I want to repent of my disobedience. I want to get right with my Lord.

If you have sinned against the Lord by your disobedience to the final command, I beg you to join me in repenting of that sin. A lost world is going to hell because of our disobedience. We dare not continue in our sin because of that lost world and because of the broken fellowship with God that disobedience causes for us. If you, too, want to return to the Lord in obedience to the final command, I'll help you. Would you join me in praying a prayer of repentance? Let's return to the Lord together!

➡ **Read the following prayer. If it expresses your desire to repent of your disobedience, pray it to the Lord; or voice your own words of repentance to the Lord.**

A Prayer of Repentance

O God, I have failed to keep Your final command. Lord Jesus, I have been disobedient to You. My disobedience is an indicator that I don't love you like I ought. I've sinned against You. Because of my sin, people have died and entered a godless eternity apart from You. Their blood is on my hands. How You must be grieved and heartbroken because of my sin. I am grieved, too.

Please forgive me. Cleanse me afresh with the shed blood of Jesus Christ, and restore me to a right fellowship with You. Take away my heart of stone and give me a tender heart of flesh to love you and to love the lost world for which you died. Give me a sense of urgency to share Christ with my world.

I do love You, and I want to obey You. Fill me with Your Holy Spirit. Guide and empower me to be Your witness to the lost world around me. Today, I surrender my life, my will, my time, and my resources to be Your servant. By your grace and help, I will no longer be disobedient to the Final Command of my Lord Jesus Christ. Amen.

➥ **If you sincerely prayed this prayer of repentance, sign your name on the line below and write today's date beside it as a reminder of your surrender to the Lord to begin obedience to the final command. Lord, today I choose to obey Your final command.**

_____

Bearing the Fruits of Repentance

God desires to see a lost world come to saving faith in Him. He longs to send revival and awakening to our land. If God's people would individually and corporately repent of this sin in large numbers and high percentages, I believe God will begin the process of spiritual awakening—of healing our land as He has promised. That repentance, however, is not just saying we're sorry for our sin. Repentance requires a new way of life in obedience to the Lord. In repentance we will begin making disciples as we go about our daily lives. We will become intentional in praying for and providing for laborers who will help us take the gospel to the ends of the earth. We will surrender our availability to our Lord should He call us to be the ones to go to the ends of the earth.

We are still a long way from being the clean and holy people God requires us to be. We cannot wait, however, until we have dealt with all the other areas of sin before we begin to deal with obedience to the final command. Surely God desires immediate and complete obedience to this command as He does to all His other commands.

Let's begin to pray that God will call for and enable repentance for all His people. Let's begin making disciples in full obedience to the final command. Let's move into obedience together!

I've prepared this action manual to help you and your church repent of your disobedience to the final command and to help you begin to obey Christ as a fruit of your repentance. Together you can join together in reaping a spiritual harvest.

➡ **Will you join me in obeying the final command of the Lord Jesus Christ?**

❏ Yes, I will obey Him. Lord, help me obey.

❏ No, I choose to live in disobedience to Christ.

❏ I'm leaning that direction, but I need a little more time to make my decision.

➡ **Will you encourage other believers in your church to join in repenting and obeying the final command together? Check any or all of the following actions you will take or write your own.**

❏ a. We're already doing this together. I've already chosen to join with others in obedience.

❏ b. I have one or more friends I will ask to join me.

❏ c. I will encourage my teacher (group leader) to guide our class in obedience.

❏ d. I will encourage my pastor to guide our whole church to practice obedience to the final command.

❏ e. Other: _____

_____

_____

THE HARVEST IS READY

Jesus describes the spiritual harvest that is ready for us:

> "Do you not say, 'Four months more and then the harvest'? I tell you, open your eyes and look at the fields! They are ripe for harvest. Even now the reaper draws his wages, even now he harvests the crop for eternal life, so that the sower and the reaper may be glad together. Thus the saying 'One sows and another reaps' is true. I sent you to reap what you have not worked for. Others have done the hard work, and you have reaped the benefits of their labor" (John 4:35-38).

Jesus also told His disciples, "'The harvest is plentiful, but the workers are few. Ask the Lord of the harvest, therefore, to send out workers into his harvest field. Go! I am sending you out…" (Luke 10:2-3).

➥ **Pause and pray according to Jesus' command. Ask Him as Lord of the harvest to call out workers who will work together in His Kingdom to bring in the spiritual harvest for eternal life. Ask Him to call out workers in your church and small group. Check here after you have prayed:** ❑

Too often, we may believe that a faithful witness for Jesus Christ must plow, plant, water, weed, and bring in the harvest all by himself or herself. Some may be gifted to do so. However, God designed the church to be a Body of Christ with many members. We all don't have the same function. We need each other. When every member does his or her part, the Body is healthy and builds itself up. When we are healthy, God adds members to the Body as it pleases Him. We need to keep the Body of Christ in mind when we think about the spiritual harvest. We all can play a part in the harvest. We can work together, each doing a part, to see the harvest brought in.

An Example of Working Together in the Harvest

Some years ago I was speaking to a group in Arkansas. A pastor related the following story of what had taken place in his church during the past six months.

A young couple from a non-church background came to faith in Christ. Soon after their conversion, their car was stolen. The pastor encouraged them to begin praying for the person who stole their car knowing that the person probably needed Christ.

A month later a fifteen-year-old boy was caught and placed in jail for the crime. This couple went to visit him in jail, but their excitement to finally meet this boy caught him a bit off guard. They showed an interest in him and in his family. They discovered that his mother was in the hospital, so they went to visit her as well.

Because of financial problems, the woman had lost their home. When the time came for her to be dismissed from the hospital, she would be homeless. This young couple took her to their own home to meet her needs and show the love of Christ. When the church learned of their actions, they decided to help. Together they secured an apartment, furnished it, and helped the woman get reestablished in a home. Overwhelmed by the love of Christ demonstrated by this couple and the church, the woman trusted Christ as her own Savior. Her son came to faith in Christ as well.

Not long after their conversion, the woman's ex-husband was paroled from prison. He came to town looking for his family. While in prison he had become a Christian himself. After studying the Bible and taking Bible correspondence courses, he sensed God was calling him to the ministry. He came home in hopes that he could be reconciled with his wife. What joy this church experienced as they watched God reunite a family in such a miraculous way. This Body of Christ in Arkansas experienced the truth that working together they could help reap a harvest.

Giftedness in the Body of Christ

As you obey the final command individually and as a church, you will find that not everyone is gifted in the same way. All have a part in obedience; all have a part in the harvest. But some will be especially gifted at a particular action. Some, for instance, will be more gifted and called to prayer. These prayer warriors will not be on the front lines, but they will be vital participants in the harvest.

Some believers are gifted at building relationships over which the gospel can flow. Others may be particularly gifted at showing love and mercy. God's life flowing through these members of the Body will draw men and women to His Son. Still others will be more gifted at introducing a person to Jesus Christ and leading him or her to genuine faith. Some in your Body will have a God-given assignment and gifting for teaching new believers to obey what God has commanded. When the church works together as the Body of Christ and filled with His Spirit, the natural result will be the winning of lost people to faith in Christ.

Mission Possible

Every church is commissioned to be a strategy center for world missions. Each one has received the final command to carry the gospel to all creation. When every member does his or her part in being a witness, planting seed, watering, weeding, and reaping, God can bring a great harvest. When every church begins to help all her members obey the final command, a whole church will be used of the Lord to carry the gospel to the ends of the earth.

Because of the latest communication technologies and because of the ease and speed of travel, this generation could very well be the one to fulfill the final command of the Lord Jesus. More than enough people and resources exist to complete the task with the Lord's empowering help. The one thing lacking is our obedience to His command. We must give absolute surrender of ourselves and our resources to the King and His authority. The King in turn promises His presence and power for us to be His faithful witnesses to the ends of the earth and the end of the age.

Church, a ripe harvest is waiting. Don't say, "let's wait four more months and then we'll join the harvest." Let the church unite and bring in the harvest in this generation. Let our united objective become:

> **A whole church reaching the whole world in this generation!**

Optional Group Activity

➡ Together with your small group or church view *The Harvest* (ordering information is on p. 99). Before you start, pray together that God will begin to show you the importance and the ways to work together in the harvest. Ask God to reveal to each individual his or her place of work in the harvest.

➡ After viewing *The Harvest* answer the following questions:

  1. What are some values of working *together* with other believers in the spiritual harvest?

  _____

  _____

  _____

  _____

  2. What do you sense God may be saying to your church regarding the community around you?

  _____

  _____

➡ In small groups pray together about what you sense God is saying to you regarding the harvest in your world. After your prayer time discuss what you sense God may be saying to your church. Make notes below.

  _____

  _____

  _____

As you join together keep in mind this encouragement from Hebrews.

> Let us hold unswervingly to the hope we profess, for he who promised is faithful. And let us consider how we may spur one another on toward love and good deeds. Let us not give up meeting together, as some are in the habit of doing, but let us encourage one another—and all the more as you see the Day approaching (Heb. 10:23-25).

1. SURVEY YOUR WORLD

"You will receive power when the Holy Spirit comes on you; and you will be my witnesses in Jerusalem, and in all Judea and Samaria, and to the ends of the earth." (Acts 1:8).

God works through relationships to draw others to Himself. You already have relationships through which He can work to touch many people in your world. Let's begin by taking a survey of your world—beginning at home and going to the ends of the earth. Begin making a list of all the people in your circles of influence. Add to this list as God brings other people to mind or as you establish new relationships. This list becomes a prayer list from which God will begin to identify your most wanted.

FAMILY AND RELATIVES

➥ **On the following pages make a list of the people in your immediate family and those who are relatives by blood or marriage. Include people whether you know their spiritual condition or not. Include:**
- husband or wife
- mother and father
- step parents
- your children
- stepchildren
- grandchildren
- sisters and brothers
- grandparents
- aunts and uncles (include great-)
- cousins
- nieces and nephews
- in-laws (mother, father, sister, brother)

Optional Reading in *Concentric Circles of Concern*

†	NAME	DATE	RELATIONSHIP/NOTE

†	Name	Date	Relationship/Note

†	NAME	DATE	RELATIONSHIP/NOTE

†	NAME	DATE	RELATIONSHIP/NOTE

Friends and Neighbors

➡ **On the following pages make a list of the people who are friends and neighbors.**

Friends: Include people to whom you are particularly close—those you spend time with, play with, care about, trust for counsel, confide in, or depend on in times of need. If you are close to the friend's family, you may include the names of his or her family members as well. Include in-town friends and out-of-town friends. You may even want to include friends of your past that you cared about deeply, even through you do not currently maintain contact.

Neighbors: Include those who live near you on your street, in your neighborhood, in your apartment building or complex, in your dorm, and so forth. This may even require that you do some research later to find out the names of those who live near you. The Lighthouses of Prayer movement suggests that you begin praying for five families on your left, five on your right, and eleven families across the street.

†	Name	Date	Relationship/Note

†	NAME	DATE	RELATIONSHIP/NOTE

COWORKERS AND ASSOCIATES

➥ **On the following pages make a list of the people who are your coworkers and associates. These would include people you see and interact with on a fairly regular basis. Include:**
  • coworkers
  • supervisors/management
  • subordinates
  • clients
  • vendors
  • other employees at your place of work
  • fellow union members
  • school classmates and teachers
  • students you teach
  • teammates in sports or recreational activities
  • fellow club members
  • fellow volunteers with whom you work regularly
  • accountants/bookkeepers
  • attorneys
  • other professionals with whom you work

SURVEY YOUR WORLD: COWORKERS & ASSOCIATES

†	NAME	DATE	RELATIONSHIP/NOTE

†	NAME	DATE	RELATIONSHIP/NOTE

ACQUAINTANCES

➡ **On the following pages make a list of the people who are your acquaintances. These are people that you may see only occasionally or for short periods. These are people you may not know well, but you know their names or their faces. Include people you know from contacts at the following places:**
  • grocery or department store
  • gas station/market
  • doctor's/dentist's office
  • club
  • fitness center/gym
  • school
  • government offices
  • library
  • barbershop or hair salon
  • mall
  • restaurant
  • other businesses
  • public transportation (bus, cab, train, plane)

†	NAME	DATE	RELATIONSHIP/NOTE

PERSON X

➥ Before you make the following list, I want you to pray and ask the Lord to identify one or more people that He would like for you to add to your lists. Person X is a person you have never met in person. This would be a person God may call you to pray for from a distance. Or it may become a person God would guide you to reach by building a relationship bridge. He may give you a burden to pray for or seek to reach a person you have yet to meet. Leave this list blank unless you sense God impressing you to add a name.

Take a moment to pray before you continue.

This list could include people who live in your town or who live a long distance from you. It may include such people as:
• civic or government leader
• school teacher or principal
• business person/leader
• business owner you see in commercials
• media personality (newspaper, TV, radio)
• entertainer
• coach or an athlete
• someone in the news
• law enforcement officer
• public servant/employee
• beggar on the street
• homeless individual you see driving to work

➥ When time permits, go back through your survey lists. If a person on your list is already one who has placed his or her faith in Jesus Christ as Lord and Savior, draw a cross (†) in the column provided. If you are not sure or if you have concerns due to a lack of spiritual fruit in his or her life, leave the column blank.

Optional Reading in *Concentric Circles of Concern*
    1. Jelly Bean, pages 105-106
    2. A Hollywood Producer, pages 47-49

†	NAME OR PEOPLE GROUP	DATE	NOTE

2. IDENTIFY YOUR MOST WANTED

Jesus' approach to doing the will of His Father was to look to see where the Father was working and join Him (see John 5:17-20). I will help you examine the people in your relationships to identify those with whom God may already be working. As God begins to reveal these to you, you will gather helpful information about each one. Then I'll give you some very specific ways to pray for these most wanted people as you watch for opportunities to join God working in their lives. You will want to review the following list regularly to see if God might identify a new person in whose life He is already working. Then you can join Him there.

➡ **1. As you keep in mind the people you have just listed in your survey, read through the following suggestions. Pray and ask God to identify for you those people on whom He wants to focus your prayers and attention. If one or more people come to mind, write his or her name on the lines provided.**

- Pray and ask God to reveal the persons of His choosing—those God wants you to carry a special burden for in prayer and action. Do you have a special burden to see a particular person come to faith in Christ? Assume that this burden is from God and the person to your list.

- As you pray through your survey lists, watch for those for whom you develop a special burden when praying.

- Watch for spiritual interest or spiritual hunger in the lives of those for whom you are praying. Are people in your survey showing a special interest in spiritual things? Are they asking questions about spiritual matters?

- Pay special attention to a person who surfaces in your survey almost unexpectedly, one that surprises you. Ask the Lord if He has brought that person to your mind because of His work in his or her life.

- Pray more intensely for people when you become aware of a special need they have. This may be God's invitation for you to show His love by meeting the need. Do you know of special needs in the lives of any of those in your survey. Pray and ask God whether He wants you involved in reaching out to this person during this time of need.

- Pay special attention to those around you when you experience a crisis together. A crisis time may give you a special opportunity to share Christ, meet a need, or demonstrate the peace of Christ or His wisdom. Have you faced a significant crisis with anyone recently?

- When you experience a broken relationship with another person, pray about how you are to seek reconciliation in a way God can use for divine purposes in the other person's life. Has anyone sinned against you in a way that you can express forgiveness and reveal God's mercy?

- Watch for people who enter your circles of influence through very unique or special circumstances. God may be bringing them into your circle of influence to introduce them to Christ through you. Did you add anyone to your list who has come into your world by unusual circumstances.

➡ 2. Reflect on the suggestions you just read. If other people's names come to mind, write them on your survey. Then begin to pray about those on your lists. Ask God to focus your attention on one or two that <u>He</u> would identify as your most wanted. If He has revealed one or more write his or her name below.

➡ 3. Take the name of this person (or persons) and start filling out a "most wanted" form for him or her on the following pages. Write down any information you already know. You can fill in the other details when you gain that information.

Name:_____ Relationship:_____

Address:_____

_____

Phone: (H)_____ (W)_____ (FAX)_____

Workplace:_____e-mail:_____

Birth Date:_____ Anniversary:_____ Other:_____

Family Members:_____

Notes: (hobbies, interests, needs) _____

_____

_____

_____

Prayer Requests: _____

_____

Introducing Jesus Christ: When?_____ How?_____

Response: _____

Name:_____ Relationship:_____

Address:_____

_____

Phone: (H)_____ (W)_____ (FAX)_____

Workplace:_____e-mail:_____

Birth Date:_____ Anniversary:_____ Other:_____

Family Members:_____

Notes: (hobbies, interests, needs) _____

_____

_____

_____

Prayer Requests: _____

_____

Introducing Jesus Christ: When?_____ How?_____

Response: _____

Name:_____ Relationship:_____

Address:_____

_____

Phone: (H)_____ (W)_____ (FAX)_____

Workplace:_____ e-mail:_____

Birth Date:_____ Anniversary:_____ Other:_____

Family Members:_____

Notes: (hobbies, interests, needs) _____

_____

_____

_____

Prayer Requests: _____

_____

Introducing Jesus Christ: When?_____ How?_____

Response: _____

Name:_____ Relationship:_____

Address:_____

_____

Phone: (H)_____ (W)_____ (FAX)_____

Workplace:_____ e-mail:_____

Birth Date:_____ Anniversary:_____ Other:_____

Family Members:_____

Notes: (hobbies, interests, needs) _____

_____

_____

_____

Prayer Requests: _____

_____

Introducing Jesus Christ: When?_____ How?_____

Response: _____

Name:_____ Relationship:_____

Address:_____

_____

Phone: (H)_____ (W)_____ (FAX)_____

Workplace:_____e-mail:_____

Birth Date:_____ Anniversary:_____ Other:_____

Family Members:_____

Notes: (hobbies, interests, needs) _____

_____

_____

_____

Prayer Requests: _____

_____

Introducing Jesus Christ: When?_____ How?_____

Response: _____

Name:_____ Relationship:_____

Address:_____

_____

Phone: (H)_____ (W)_____ (FAX)_____

Workplace:_____e-mail:_____

Birth Date:_____ Anniversary:_____ Other:_____

Family Members:_____

Notes: (hobbies, interests, needs) _____

_____

_____

_____

Prayer Requests: _____

_____

Introducing Jesus Christ: When?_____ How?_____

Response: _____

Name:_____ Relationship:_____

Address:_____

_____

Phone: (H)_____ (W)_____ (FAX)_____

Workplace:_____e-mail:_____

Birth Date:_____ Anniversary:_____ Other:_____

Family Members:_____

Notes: (hobbies, interests, needs) _____

_____

_____

_____

Prayer Requests: _____

_____

Introducing Jesus Christ: When?_____ How?_____

Response: _____

Name:_____ Relationship:_____

Address:_____

_____

Phone: (H)_____ (W)_____ (FAX)_____

Workplace:_____e-mail:_____

Birth Date:_____ Anniversary:_____ Other:_____

Family Members:_____

Notes: (hobbies, interests, needs) _____

_____

_____

_____

Prayer Requests: _____

_____

Introducing Jesus Christ: When?_____ How?_____

Response: _____

Name:_____ Relationship:_____

Address:_____

_____

Phone: (H)_____ (W)_____ (FAX)_____

Workplace:_____e-mail:_____

Birth Date:_____ Anniversary:_____ Other:_____

Family Members:_____

Notes: (hobbies, interests, needs) _____

_____

_____

_____

Prayer Requests: _____

_____

Introducing Jesus Christ: When?_____ How?_____

Response: _____

Name:_____ Relationship:_____

Address:_____

_____

Phone: (H)_____ (W)_____ (FAX)_____

Workplace:_____e-mail:_____

Birth Date:_____ Anniversary:_____ Other:_____

Family Members:_____

Notes: (hobbies, interests, needs) _____

_____

_____

_____

Prayer Requests: _____

_____

Introducing Jesus Christ: When?_____ How?_____

Response: _____

PRAYING FOR THOSE WHO NEED TO TRUST CHRIST

Prayer is one of the greatest weapons in a Christian's work for Christ. Some people will have a special calling to pray for others. I have some prayer warriors who pray for me for hours when they know I'll be speaking. Your church will have some with that kind of calling. Even if you are not called to that level of prayer, you still have an assignment to pray for those God has brought into your world. The following list is intended to give you some suggestions of ways to pray for God to work. As you pray for your most wanted people, ask the Lord to guide your praying. Ask Him to open your spiritual eyes and ears so He can reveal to you special ways to pray specifically. Watch for those in your church who are especially called to intercession and invite them to pray specifically for those you are seeking to reach.

➡ **Keep in mind the name of the person or persons God may already have identified as your most wanted. You may want to place a bookmark at this spot (or fold down a corner of the page) so you can turn to it easily as you pray for your most wanted.**

Now read through the following suggestions for prayer. Check those that seem to be meaningful or that apply to his or her circumstances. Pray and ask the Lord to guide you as you read this list.

❑ Bring the person to recognize and understand his emptiness and purposelessness in life. Bring him to the end of himself so that he will turn to You.

❑ Cause him to hunger and thirst for more in life.

❑ Bring him to understand the truth of his condition without Christ and to understand what Christ has done for his salvation.

❑ Bring conviction of sin. Allow the consequences of his sin to cause him to desire a different life. Let him become fed up with his life as it is.

❑ Jesus, reveal the Father to him.

❑ Father, exalt Jesus in his eyes.

❑ Father, draw him to Yourself and Your Son Jesus.

❑ Guide and create circumstances that create a need, then show Your love through meeting needs through me or others of Your people.

❑ Bring godly people into his life that will influence Him for Christ.

❑ Prepare circumstances in his relationships where a Christian (me if you choose) will have the opportunity to forgive him and thus reveal something of your mercy.

❑ Open his ears to hear Your call.

❑ Allow him to see the unity and love of Your people in a way that he is convinced that Jesus must be sent from You. Convince him that Jesus is indeed the Savior of the world.

❑ Prepare his life to receive the planting of Your Word.

❑ Protect him from Satan's attempts to blind him and steal away the Word that has been sown.

❑ Reduce the cares of the world around him that could choke the seed planted.

❑ Raise up intercessors in behalf of this person. Guide my praying for him.

❑ Reveal to me the time and the way for me to share a witness about you and to tell him about the good news of salvation.

❑ Bring him under the hearing and influence of Your Word through teaching or preaching. Create in him an openness to listen.

❑ Create opportunities for him to hear a witness for Christ from several different trusted sources. Use the timing and diversity of these witnesses to convince him that You are the Author behind them all.

❑ Cause him to recognize his need for a Savior.

❑ Lord, do whatever it takes to cause this person to seek after You. Break the hardness of his heart toward You.

➥ **As you pray, write below additional ways or Scriptures God guides you to pray for those who need to place their faith in Jesus Christ as Savior.**

_____
_____
_____
_____
_____
_____

Optional Reading in *Concentric Circles of Concern*

3. RECONCILE
BROKEN RELATIONSHIPS

Broken relationships can hinder your willingness and effectiveness to be a witness to a person or group. These relationships must be reconciled not only for you to be right with God, but also as a means of preparing a clear channel through which the gospel about Jesus Christ can flow. You should start by reconciling relationships with those who are in your family and those who are brothers and sisters in Christ. As you pray and examine relationships with your Most Wanted, God will help you know when a relationship with an unbeliever needs to be reconciled.

THE PARABLE OF THE PCV PIPE

(Pastor Bill Elliff gave me the seed thoughts for this parable.) Your life is like a PVC pipe (or any kind of pipe). It is a channel through which Jesus—the Living Water—flows. On one end of your "pipe" you must be connected to God by a saving relationship with Him through Jesus Christ, your Savior. On the other end of your pipe you are connected to other people through relationships. God's desire and mission is to work through your life in such a way that others will come to saving faith in His Son—that they would be reconciled to God. We could illustrate your life like this:

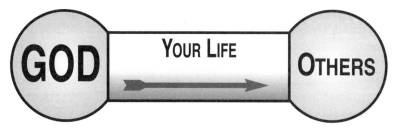

A Clogged Pipe

Some people have a problem with their pipe. It is clogged up and the Living Water cannot flow through it as intended. Sin can clog up your pipeline by shutting off your access to the power and filling presence of the Holy Spirit. God's holiness and righteousness cannot be revealed (flow) through a dirty life.

Love of pleasure and love of the world or the things of the world can clog up your pipe. The Scriptures say, "Do not love the world or anything in the world. If anyone loves the world, the love of the Father is not in him" (1 John 2:15). God's first and greatest command to us is this: "'Love the Lord your God with all your heart and with all your soul and with all your mind'" (Matt. 22:37). The love of God cannot flow through a life that is filled with the love of other people, activities, or things in place of a wholehearted love for God. Love of self can also keep the Living Water from flowing.

If your pipe is clogged by sin, self, or the love of something that takes the place of your love for God, you need to get your pipe cleaned out. Clean out your "pipe" by:
• confessing and repenting of your sin,
• daily denying yourself in order to follow Christ, and
• putting away "idols of the heart" and returning to your first love for God.

A Capped Pipe

Another problem can exist with the flow of Living Water through your PVC pipe. If you have a broken relationship with a person, you have a cap on the end of your pipe that stops or limits the flow. The person may not be willing to listen to you or receive the Living Water from your life. Two kinds of broken relationships may be present in your relationships with others.

In one case you may have sinned against the other person or group. Jesus gave this command to you:

> "'If you are offering your gift at the altar and there remember that your brother has something against you, leave your gift there in front of the altar. First go and be reconciled to your brother; then come and offer your gift'" (Matt. 5:23-24).

Even your worship is not acceptable to God if you have a broken relationship that has not been reconciled. Reconciling that relationship by seeking forgiveness and, if necessary, making restitution removes the cap off your pipe so the Living Water can flow once again.

The other kind of broken relationship is where you have been offended (or sinned against) by the other person. If you are withholding forgiveness, your pipe will be capped. If that is the case, Jesus has two things to say to you:

> "'If you forgive men when they sin against you, your heavenly Father will also forgive you. But if you do not forgive men their sins, your Father will not forgive your sins'" (Matt. 6:14-15).
> "'When you stand praying, if you hold anything against anyone, forgive him, so that your Father in heaven may forgive you your sins'" (Mark 11:25).

When you have been sinned against, forgive. This will uncap your pipe so that God's grace and love can flow through your life. Forgiveness is a command, not an option. The wonderful thing about this command is that the Holy Spirit of Christ in you can enable you to forgive in obedience to the command. When you forgive when the other person does not deserve it, you reveal the grace and forgiveness of God—so forgive and uncap your pipe.

> **When you forgive another person or group you are probably more like Christ than at any other time.**

A Clean and Clear Pipe

When your pipe is clean and clear of all clogs, the Living Water can flow through you. When relationships with others are right and clear, they become opportunities for you to reveal Christ and His grace, mercy, and love. What's the condition of your "PVC pipe"? The following exercises are designed to help you identify areas where you may need to reconcile broken relationships. These have been copied from *Come to the Lord's Table* (Claude King, © 2001). If you have already worked through these activities, review them now.

➥ **Which kind of "pipe" best describes your life? Circle one:**
    clogged   capped   clean and clear

> **Optional Reading in *Concentric Circles of Concern***
> 1. Jim and His Father, pages 7-8
> 2. Reconciled at Home First, page 21
> 3. Reconciled to an Absentee Father, pages 23-24
> 4. Jerry Craig and Uncle Ben, pages 89-92

YOUR VERTICAL RELATIONSHIP WITH GOD

➡ **Prayerfully read through the following list of sins and areas of sin. Ask the Lord to reveal to you any area in which you have not turned away from sin and experienced His cleansing. Ask Him to show you any sin that is hindering your fellowship with Him. You may want to check any that God identifies, so you can deal with your sin seriously.**

❑ unbelief—not believing God will keep His word
❑ rebellion—disobedience, not letting Christ be Lord of all, living my own way
❑ pride/arrogance—thinking more highly of myself than I ought
❑ bitterness, unforgiveness
❑ sins of the tongue—gossip, slander, murmuring, lying, cursing, filthy speech, vain talk, obscenity
❑ dishonesty, deceit
❑ mental impurity
❑ addiction to harmful or illegal substances
❑ addiction to pornography
❑ sexual immorality
❑ stealing, cheating, embezzlement
❑ anger, hatred, malice, rage, uncontrolled temper
❑ idolatry—worshipping another god, or loving something or someone more than you love God
❑ poor stewardship of time and resources
❑ prayerlessness
❑ taking unfair advantage of others
❑ disobedience to the clear commands of the Lord
❑ injustice, failing to defend the oppressed
❑ murder, hating your brother without a cause
❑ causing strife and dissension in the church
❑ worshipping with your lips when your heart is far away from loving the Lord
❑ leaving your first love for Christ
Others:
❑ _____
❑ _____

This is certainly not a complete list of sins. You can miss God's standards in many ways through your thoughts, actions, and words. Develop a heart that is ready to confess and repent at the slightest whisper of conviction from the Holy Spirit. If God has convicted you of sin, take action now to get right with Him.

- Confess: agree with God that you have sinned.
- Repent: turn away from your sin and turn to God to live His way.
- Seek the Lord's forgiveness and cleansing.
- Show your repentance by a changed life/deeds.

➡ **Now, ask the Lord to reveal any "idols of the heart" that may have led you away from your wholehearted love for the Lord. These may be things that are not evil in themselves, but they have captured too much of your love. You may not need to throw these away, but you may need to give them away or sell them to break their hold on your love. Only the Lord can reveal to you whether something has captured your love. He will also help you understand what you must do to break their ties to your heart.**

Ask Him to help you. One way you might test something is to ask yourself, "If God, Himself, asked me to give this up, would I resist Him or have a struggle to do it?" If you are holding on too tight, the item may be an "idol of the heart." These things could include:

- Hobbies or collections (the idol may be things or activities)
- A material object that you treasure too dearly
- Material things that consume far too much of your time using them or maintaining them
- Things you have to impress others or that cause you to feel arrogant or condescending toward others
- Things you have purchased for yourself that you know God didn't want you to have
- Activities you love that consume too much of your time and may even keep you from your time with God or from serving Him obediently

➡ **Make a list of the things or activities God brings to your mind. If you have questions about whether an item has become an idol in your heart, talk to the Lord about it until you have peace about how God sees it. If something comes to mind and you still are not sure about whether it is an idol in your heart, write it down with a question mark. Continue praying about the matter until you have some clear direction from the Lord. Use extra paper if you need more space.**

_____

_____

_____

_____

_____

➡ **If you have identified idols of your heart pray about the following and check each one when you finish.**

  ❑ Confess to the Lord that you have given your love and attention to these items or activities. Agree with Him that you have sinned.

  ❑ Ask Him to forgive and cleanse you.

  ❑ Ask Him to set you free from your love for these things. Remember the height from which you have fallen and return to Him as your first love.

  ❑ Pledge to Him your renewed loyalty, love, and desire to please Him and obey Him.

Your Horizontal Relationship with Others

➡ **Read through the following list of relationships that may need to be made right in your life. Place a check beside any item that describes a relationship you have that needs reconciliation.**

  ❑ Have I mistreated anyone by my actions or with my words that I have not gone to the person and asked forgiveness?

  ❑ Have I stolen anything from a person, an organization, a business, my employer, or anyone else and not gone back and made restitution?

  ❑ Do I hold a grudge or bitterness in my heart toward anyone?

  ❑ Have I gossiped about or slandered another person?

  ❑ Have I borrowed anything that I have failed to return?

  ❑ Has God impressed me to do something to meet another person's needs and I have failed to obey Him?

  ❑ Have I done anything illegal which I need to confess?

  ❑ Have I lied to anyone or falsified information?

  ❑ Have I hurt someone because of an immoral act and covered it up rather than clean and clear it up?

  ❑ Am I currently in a wrong or immoral relationship with anyone?

❑ Have I been guilty of not expressing gratitude to a person or group when I certainly should have? Am I taking someone for granted and need to show my gratitude in words and deeds?

❑ Have I allowed jealously, envy, or resentment to have a negative effect on the way I have related to a person or group?

❑ Have I allowed pride to keep me from relating to a person who needed a friend?

❑ Have I sinned against God and another person or group by committing any of the following sins?

❑ anger	❑ anxiety	❑ arguing
❑ arrogance	❑ bitterness	❑ blasphemy
❑ boasting	❑ coarse talking	❑ conceit
❑ complaining	❑ competition	❑ covetousness
❑ cursing	❑ critical spirit	❑ deception
❑ unforgiveness	❑ discord	❑ disorder
❑ divisiveness	❑ envy	❑ factions
❑ faultfinding	❑ fear	❑ fits of rage
❑ gossip	❑ greed	❑ grumbling
❑ hatred	❑ hypocrisy	❑ impatience
❑ impurity	❑ independence	❑ injustice
❑ insensitivity	❑ jealousy	❑ lack of love
❑ lies	❑ malice	❑ oppression
❑ persecution	❑ prejudice	❑ pride
❑ quarreling	❑ resentment	❑ revenge
❑ rudeness	❑ slander	❑ stereotyping
❑ strife	❑ unbelief	❑ self-seeking

❑ judgmental spirit   ❑ intolerance of differences
❑ party spirit (factions)   ❑ lawsuits among believers
❑ protecting "turf"   ❑ keeping record of wrongs
❑ provoking one another ❑ self-centeredness
❑ self-righteousness   ❑ a controlling spirit
❑ selfish ambition   ❑ struggle for control
❑ spirit of superiority   ❑ delighting in downfall of a brother

If the Holy Spirit has brought to your mind any relationships that are broken, decide now to make those relationships right.

➡ **List below any persons or groups whom you have offended by your sin and need to be forgiven and reconciled.**

❑ _____

❑ _____

❑ _____
❑ _____
❑ _____
❑ _____

Perhaps others have sinned against you. Have you forgiven them as Jesus has commanded. If you hold a grudge, bitterness, or an emotional ill will or hatred toward a person, you probably have not forgiven.

➡ **List below any persons or groups who have offended you or sinned against you that you have not yet forgiven. If you have a question about whether you have forgiven, add the person's name to your list anyway.**

❑ _____
❑ _____
❑ _____
❑ _____

If you have listed persons or groups on the previous above, you need to reconcile the broken relationship. This may take some time. Here are some suggestions to help you respond to those who have surfaced on your lists.

If You Are the Offender[1]

1. Pray and ask God for help in thorough repentance.
2. Go to make things right out of obedience to God.
3. Put the hardest person first on your list.
4. Confess your sin to God and to those directly affected by the sin.
5. Don't apologize. Ask for forgiveness.
6. Go in person (best choice), call by phone (second choice), or write a letter (last resort).
7. Don't reflect negatively on the other person or his actions or attitudes. Deal only with your part of the offense.
8. Make restitution (pay for the offense) when appropriate.
9. Don't expect to receive a positive response every time. Continue to pray for and seek reconciliation with an unforgiving person. Jesus command is: "Be reconciled."

If You Are the One Offended[1]

1. Forgive the offender. Forgiveness is a command, not an option: "Bear with each other and forgive whatever grievances you may have against one another. Forgive as the Lord

forgave you" (Col. 3:13). "'If you do not forgive men their sins, your Father will not forgive your sins'" (Matt. 6:15).

2. You cannot forgive and love in your own strength. The Holy Spirit of Christ in you can enable you to forgive and love. Ask Him to enable you to forgive.

3. Forgiveness is a choice of your will, not the result of a feeling. You must choose to forgive.

4. Begin to pray for God to work in the person's life for his or her good. Continue praying until you can do so with a sincere desire to see God bless the person for his or her good.

5. Make an investment in the person who wronged you by returning good for evil. Ask God to guide you in this response and in the timing of it. Ask Him what you can do to meet a need or show love.

Other Teaching on Forgiveness

- Forgiveness is fully releasing another from the debt of the offense.
- The person who forgives is the one who has to pay the price of forgiveness. Jesus paid the price for you.
- You are never more like Jesus than when you forgive and show grace and mercy. Being offended provides you with the invitation to reveal Christ to the offender by your forgiveness.
- Forgiveness does not mean that the offense was not wrong.
- Forgiveness is not permission for the offender to do it again. It does not require you to place yourself in harms way again.
- Forgiveness does not mean that you will fully forget. You choose not to hold the offense against the person any longer.
- How much do you forgive? "Seventy times seven" (Matt. 18:21-22, KJV). In other words: forgive an unlimited amount.
- Jesus said, "'If [your brother] sins against you seven times in a day, and seven times comes back to you and says, "I repent," forgive him'" (Luke 17:4). In other words: even if the offender really doesn't repent and change his ways, you still forgive.
- Even if the person doesn't believe he's wrong, forgive. Jesus set the model for us on the cross when He prayed for those who were killing Him, "'Father, forgive them, for they do not know what they are doing'" (Luke 23:34).

---

[1]I've been influenced greatly in these matters by Life Action Ministries, P. O. Box 31, Buchanan, Michigan 49107-0031 (www.LifeAction.org). They have valuable resources to guide you in reconciling relationships.

4. REVEAL GOD'S MERCY AND LOVE

You are probably never more like Jesus than when you choose to forgive. When you forgive a person who doesn't deserve it, you show God's grace (undeserved favor). That is what Jesus perfectly did on the cross for us. When you reconcile relationships with others the life and love of God can flow through your life.

Now you are in a position to reveal even more of God by showing His mercy and love. *Mercy* is a demonstration of empathy toward a person in need by meeting the need. Mercy and love go together. God-like love seeks the very best for another person. Oscar Thompson, in *Concentric Circles of Concern*, defines love like this:

> "Love is meeting needs."

Begin to watch and pray for opportunities to reveal God to those around you and especially to your most wanted. Where relationships are shallow, you can begin building relationship bridges over which God's love can travel.

➡ **Mark the following statements "T" (True) or "F" (False).**

___ 1. When I reconcile broken relationships with others, my life can become a clean channel for God's love.

___ 2. When I forgive others who don't deserve to be forgiven, I show them what God's grace is like.

___ 3. When I love another person like God loves, I will seek to meet his needs.

(Answers: T–1, 2, 3)

Reveal Mercy and Love at Home and at Church

God has given us families and churches in which we are to display mercy and love. Begin praying for and with other believers. Learn to love deeply as you minister to the needs of believers in your family and church. Practice forgiveness and reconciling relationships with other believers with whom you have experienced a broken relationship. This response to believers is essential for a healthy relationship with God. As you apply God's principles for relationships with other believers, God equips, strengthens, and expands your capacity to love and forgive a lost world for the sake of Christ.

I had a friend whose wife was diagnosed with Lou Gehrig's Disease. She very gradually began losing muscle control in her arms, then legs, and eventually all her muscle functions began shutting down. As the disease progressed, she was unable to function without assistance. They were members of a relatively young church with several hundred members. The people began to express their love for Tim, Janiece, and their young children. They helped with cooking, laundry, and house cleaning. They ran errands and took care of the lawn so Tim could devote time to his wife and family. Toward the end of her life, Janiece required constant attention. People helped 24 hours a day. This church expressed their love deeply.

I attended her memorial service. It was a beautiful testimony of a godly woman. As the pastor spoke, he posed a question: "I wonder why God has given our young church this opportunity to love so deeply?" After the service, the church provided a meal for family and out-of-town guests. I gave the pastor a copy of *Concentric Circles of Concern* and explained what I sensed God was doing. I said, "Bill, Oscar says that God gives us families and churches to practice and demonstrate our love. God has taken this church to deep levels of genuine love as you have cared for Tim and Janiece. Now He wants to ask you, "Will you love a lost world that much so they can come to faith in Christ?"

Bill clapped his hands and said, "That's it. That's my sermon for Sunday." It was the Christmas season. The previous Sunday Bill preached on the incarnation of Christ where Jesus became flesh to live among us. He explained that he wanted to challenge the church to become the incarnation of Christ to their world as the new Body of Christ—the church. The following Sunday, Bill reminded and commended his church for the sacrificial love they had shown to this family. Then he posed the question, "Would you be willing to love lost people in our community just as much in order to lead them to saving faith in Jesus Christ?"

Brothers and Sisters in Christ, that is <u>our</u> invitation. Jesus shed his blood and suffered a humiliating death for you and me. He has provided forgiveness and salvation for all the world. He desires that none perish and that all come to repentance (2 Pet. 3:9).

Jesus is in heaven now. He has placed His Holy Spirit in us to empower us to be effective and powerful witnesses for Jesus. We are the Body of Christ for our world. The harvest and the success of the Kingdom depend on our obedience to the final command. We will show the world what Christ is like by our love for one another. On the night before He died on the cross, Jesus gave us this command: "'Love one another. As I have loved you, so you must love one another. By this all men will know that you are my disciples, if you love one another'" (John 13:34-35). Let's reveal God to a lost world by loving one another. Then we can give ourselves to sacrificial love of a lost world. Paul said:

> Let us not become weary in doing good, for at the proper time we will reap a harvest if we do not give up. Therefore, as we have opportunity, let us do good to all people, especially to those who belong to the family of believers (Gal. 6:9-10).

➡ **Mark the following statements "T" (True) or "F" (False).**

___ 1. My witness to lost people is not affected by whether I love my family and my brothers and sisters in Christ.

___ 2. Jesus commanded me to love my brothers and sisters in Christ in the same way He loved me.

___ 3. The way the lost world will know we are Jesus' disciples is by our knowledge of Scripture and the effective way we proclaim our doctrines.

___ 4. The harvest does not depend on me. I can leave that work for somebody else to do, and God will still be pleased with me.

___ 5. We can show the world what Jesus is like by the way we love one another.

(Answers: T–2, 5; F–1, 3,4)

➡ **Is there someone in your immediate family on whom God would have you practice mercy and love? Read the following list. Check those areas that you sense God is calling you to reveal love and mercy in a specific way toward a family member. Check all that apply.**

❑ show grace and mercy by forgiving and restoring a broken relationship

❑ show love by meeting a need (or needs)

❑ pray for and begin by asking, "How can I pray for you?"

❑ cultivate a closer relationship by building a relationship bridge

➡ **Write the name of the family member and briefly describe the project, need, opportunity, or action planned.**

➡ Is there someone in your church to whom God would have you show mercy and love? Read the following list. Check those areas that you sense God is calling you to reveal love and mercy in a specific way toward a church member or other brother or sister in Christ. Check all that apply.

❑ show grace and mercy by forgiving and restoring a broken relationship

❑ show love by meeting a need (or needs)

❑ pray for and begin by asking, "How can I pray for you?"

❑ cultivate a closer relationship by building a relationship bridge

➡ Write the name of the church member (or church members) and briefly describe the project, need, opportunity, or action planned.

> **Optional Reading in** *Concentric Circles of Concern*
> 1. A Homesick Wife, pages 165-166
> 2. A Husband's Needs, pages 166-167
> 3. Loving the One Who Bugs You, pages 169-171

Reveal God's Love by Meeting Needs

As you begin to reach out to your most wanted people, love them in the name of Christ. As you pray for them, watch to see if God makes you aware of a need that you can meet. That may be God's invitation for you to join Him as He works in that person's life. When the need is beyond your resources to meet, pray and ask the Lord to reveal to you how to be involved. God may provide the resources in an unexpected way, or He may involve others in your church to help meet the need.

➡ Fill in the blank to complete this definition of love.

"Love is _____ needs.

➡ **Read the following list of possible needs and place a check beside any that help you think of a way you may be able to show love to one of your most wanted.**

❑ basic human needs like food, water, clothes, or shelter

❑ basic skills training: like reading, math skills, verbal skills, parenting skills, computer skills, or other job skills

❑ car repair

❑ comfort in a time of grief

❑ defense against oppression

❑ encouragement to break free from a destructive habit

❑ financial counseling or money management skills

❑ financial resources to provide for basic family needs

❑ friendship, companionship, attention

❑ health or dental care

❑ help at reconciling a broken relationship with others

❑ help with childcare

❑ a break from overwhelming childcare pressures

❑ help with house or lawn work due to physical limitations

❑ a job, or employment opportunity

❑ justice

❑ assistance in working through government "red tape"

❑ learning English as a second language

❑ manual help to do a job that the person cannot do alone

❑ marriage counseling or enrichment

❑ material things that the person needs but can't afford

❑ an opportunity to experience success or personal fulfillment

❑ prayer for a felt need

❑ protection and security from an unsafe environment

❑ someone to talk to, confide in, seek counsel from

❑ time for husband and wife to get away from the children for some couple time

❑ transportation

❑ tutoring (like help in getting a GED)

❑ a visit when they are in the hospital, nursing home, prison

❑ wise counsel for critical decision making

➡ **If God has brought to your mind a need in the life of one of your most wanted, write his or her name below and describe the need. How might you be involved in meeting that need?**

_____

_____

The Need May Point You to Your Most Wanted Person

God may use a variety of approaches to involve you in reaching people for salvation. One is described above. In that case you have prayed and identified people that need Christ. Then you begin watching for a need so you can show God's love by meeting the need.

The opposite sequence may be used by God as well. You may become aware of a need in the life of a person who may not even be on your survey list—this might be a "Person X" that you have never met before. As you see the need and respond in love, God works through that love to draw the person to Himself. This may then become one of your most wanted because God is showing you a place where He is at work.

➡ **Review the list of needs on the previous pages. Do you know of people around your life who have needs like these? Certainly you do. As people come to mind, pray and ask God if He is leading you to show His love by meeting one of those needs. If God seems to be impressing upon you a person with a need to meet, write the name and need below.**

> **Optional Reading in *Concentric Circles of Concern***
> 1. Jerry and the Motorcycle Mirror, pages 151-152
> 2. Paving the Church Parking Lot, page 143

How Can I Pray for You?

Another way to express love to a person is to pray for him or her. But the way the person will feel or experience that kind of love best is to hear you pray for his or her need. Consider asking a person this question: *"How can I pray for You?"* When he responds with a need for prayer, pray with the person at that moment. You will be amazed at the way prayer communicates concern, love, compassion, and caring. Make a mental or written note and continue to pray for the person's need. Watch for ways God may call you to be the answer to the prayer by meeting a need or by connecting the person with someone else who can meet the need.

➡ **What is a question you can use to initiate an opportunity to show love through prayer? Write it below.**

The final command essentially says, "As you go..." Keep your eyes and ears open throughout the day for needs and opportunities to pray. Sometimes I've seen a person with a heavy countenance. By the look on his or her face, I could tell something was wrong. If I have a relationship, or the situation is appropriate, I just say something like this: *"I sense that you may be carrying a heavy burden today. Is there some way I can pray for you?"* To keep from prying, I might say, "I sense that you may be carrying a heavy burden today. May I pray for you?" Then I just ask the Lord to minister to their deepest need. After such a prayer, the person often opens up with the burden behind their troubled expressions. Then I pray again but more specifically.

When you go to lunch or break, watch for the person sitting alone. He may need your friendship or prayers today. Listen for the coworker who talks about a problem or need. Then respond, "Would you mind if I pray for you about that?"

Prayer Station

YWAM (Youth With A Mission) in Metro New York City introduced me to using this prayer concept in a public outreach. They set up a "Prayer Station" on the sidewalk especially during special events like New Year's Eve in Times Square. The prayer station is a table with a banner over it reading "Prayer Station." Volunteer intercessors wear brightly colored vests reading "Prayer Changes Things." People on each end of the block hand out flyers inviting people to receive prayer for their felt needs.

At first, they were scared to try it in a sophisticated place like New York City. But they found many people would stop for prayer who would show no interest in evangelistic type interaction. People out there are hurting. After a person gets prayed for by a caring Christian, many open their lives wide to the gospel. Others willingly accept a gospel tract or Bible portion. Others come back after their prayers are answered to find out more about the God to whom you prayed.

You can find out more about prayer stations by writing to: YWAM Metro Inc., 70 New York Ave., Smithtown, NY 11787 or by e-mail at info@ywam-ny.com.

Build Relationship Bridges

If your relationship to a most wanted person is shallow, you may need to spend time cultivating the relationship before you will be in a better position to show God's love by meeting a need. This relationship becomes a channel through which the love of Christ can flow to another. Paul did this in order to reach people for Christ. He said,

> Though I am free and belong to no man, I make myself a slave to everyone, *to win as many as possible.* To the Jews I became like a Jew, to win the Jews. To those under the law I became like one under the law,... so as to win those under the law. To those not having the law I became like one not having the law,... so as to win those not having the law. To the weak I became weak, to win the weak. I have become all things to all men so that by all possible means I might save some. I do all this for the sake of the gospel, that I may share in its blessings. (1 Cor. 9:19-23)

God may call you to take on a project to reach a particular group of people, not just one individual. I heard of a couple who had a wayward son. The son played in a rock band at a local nightclub. Rather than fight with their son to change his behavior, they decided to influence his peers for Christ. They went to the nightclub regularly and ordered soft drinks. As they began interacting with the people who attended the club, they had opportunities to listen, to counsel, to show concern, to pray. Before long they became "Mom and Pop" to these wayward children from other people's homes. By building a relationship with the regulars, they began to have opportunity to introduce these people to Jesus Christ.

God may call you to invest time, energy, and resources to reach one person for Christ. As you develop a caring relationship with the person, he or she becomes more responsive to receive the message of Christ when you do share it. This relationship, however, is not just a means of manipulating a decision. It should become a relationship of love that continues as a person grows in Christ.

I was visiting in the home of a retired business executive in Texas. I was teaching about the Final Command in his church. I think he was struggling to understand how he might get involved in reaching people for Christ. He lived on a golf course. I asked him about his golf game. He and several of his Christian friends got together two or three times a week to play golf, but sometimes they had trouble making up a foursome. I suggested that this group of men begin building relationship bridges to the others who were retiring near the golf course. The could regularly start with three and ask the Lord to help them reach out to a fourth person who needed to know Christ. You would have thought he a little child with a new toy. Suddenly he realized how easily he could begin obeying the final command as he went about his normal routine.

➡ **Read through the following list of ways you can culti-vate relationships. Check any that may be ways you would choose to build relationship bridges.**

❏ developing an interest and participation in the same hobby or recreational activity

❏ spending time with the person over lunch or a break

❏ inviting the person into your world for some event or special activity

❏ inviting the person into your home for dinner

❏ expressing interest during times of joy or celebration (marriage, birth of a baby, graduation, job promotion, etc.)

❏ working together on a common interest project or working together for a common cause

❏ sending cards (birthday, anniversary, sympathy) or writing notes

❏ vacationing, camping, or picnicking together with each others families

❏ or by demonstrating love by meeting needs (as described earlier)

❏ Others: _____

_____

_____

_____

➡ **Review your list of most wanted people or your survey of relationships. Ask the Lord to guide you to build a relationship bridge with one or more people so that you can bring them across that bridge to a relationship with Jesus Christ. If a person comes to mind, write his or her name below and a way you might begin building a bridge to him or her.**

_____

_____

_____

_____

_____

5. INTRODUCE JESUS CHRIST

Not long after the Jewish leaders had crucified Jesus, Peter and John healed a crippled beggar in the name and by the power of Jesus. A crowd gathered to see this wonderful miracle. They took the opportunity to tell the people about Jesus Christ—the Savior. The Jewish leaders arrested them and put them in jail.

Can you imagine what must have gone through their minds, knowing that this same group had killed Jesus? The next day they were commanded to never preach in the name of Jesus again. They responded, "We cannot help speaking about what we have seen and heard" (Acts 4:20). When they were released, Peter and John went back to report to the rest of the church. They held a prayer meeting, but they didn't pray for protection. No, they prayed: "Lord, consider their threats and enable your servants to speak your word with great boldness" (Acts 4:29).

Peter and John had experienced salvation. They had experienced the life and teaching of Jesus for over three years. Now they were filled with the Holy Spirit and knew the power of the resurrection. They couldn't help telling everybody about this salvation that Jesus offered to all. Jesus had come to set people free from the bondage of sin. That was good news!

Our world needs to hear that good news—the gospel of Jesus Christ. Your family, relatives, friends, and neighbors need to be set free from the bondage of sin. They need to experience the hope, purpose, and abundant life that come through Jesus.

➡ **What are some of the reasons the people on your survey need Jesus Christ. Check any that you know apply.**

❑ broken relationships	❑ bitterness and unforgiveness
❑ no peace	❑ no purpose in life
❑ destined for hell	❑ no genuine love
❑ bondage to a sin/vice	❑ lonely
❑ spiritual emptiness	❑ emotional brokenness

❑ no hope for circumstances or the future
❑ grieving over lost loved ones as those who have no hope
❑ need fellowship of the Body of Christ
❑ Others: _____

_____
_____
_____

Ministry and prayer alone will not bring a person to faith in Jesus Christ. A person must hear the gospel about Jesus Christ and make a choice to die to self, receive Christ's atonement for sin, and live to Christ. People must hear and respond to the gospel message. Paul wrote:

> "Everyone who calls on the name of the Lord will be saved."
>
> How, then, can they call on the one they have not believed in? And how can they believe in the one of whom they have not heard? And how can they hear without someone preaching to them? And how can they preach unless they are sent?...
>
> Consequently, faith comes from hearing the message, and the message is heard through the word of Christ (Rom. 10:13-17).

Someone has to introduce people to Jesus Christ and the message of salvation. Paul wrote to Philemon and said, "I pray that you may be active in sharing your faith, so that you will have a full understanding of every good thing we have in Christ" (Philemon 6). That is my prayer for you and your church so that you, too, will fully understand all the good things we have because of Christ. You cannot experience that without sharing your faith actively. If your "PVC pipe" is not flowing to others, your experience of Living Water will stagnate.

If you have personally experienced salvation and new life in Christ, you are a qualified witness. A witness is one who tells about what he or she has observed and experienced. I will help you identify some practical ways you can introduce others to Jesus Christ. You can be His witness because of the Holy Spirit He has placed in you. But some people in your church are especially gifted at helping people understand the gospel and come to saving faith. I also will help you understand ways you can work together with other members of the Body of Christ to see people introduced to the Savior. Together with the Body of Christ, you will begin introducing people to your Savior.

Some Ways People Are Introduced to Jesus Christ

People may be introduced to Jesus Christ in a variety of ways. For instance:

1. Some read or hear the gospel through media like a track, a book, a Bible or Scripture portion, on the radio or television, or through a movie or video message. God's Spirit works in their hearts through the message and they come to faith in Christ.
2. Some attend a group Bible study, Sunday School or other class, worship services, evangelistic meetings, or some other type of meeting. They hear the gospel taught and preached. God works through teachers and preachers or evangelists to lead them to personal faith in Jesus Christ.
3. Some hear a verbal testimony and the message of the gospel from an individual who intentionally seeks to lead the person to faith in Christ. God works through the person's testimony and the gospel message to draw the person to faith in His Son Jesus Christ.
4. Some grow up in a Christian family or environment where they hear and are taught the gospel. They see it lived out in the lives of people around them. God works through these means until the time comes when they come to place their personal faith in Jesus Christ.
5. Some witness a miraculous demonstration of God's power to change lives much like the crowd that gathered around Peter and John in Acts 3 and 4. When they hear the explanation of what Jesus has done and what He can do for them, they respond by believing in Christ.
6. Sometimes God visits a person in a more dramatic and personal way like He did with Paul on the road to Damascus (Acts 9:1-19). Knowing that God is revealing Himself in the appeal, this person chooses to respond. Still he or she needs to hear the gospel.
7. Still others experience a variety of the means mentioned above as God draws them to faith in His Son.

> ➡ **Who introduced you to Jesus Christ as Savior, or how did you come to understand that you need to turn to Christ in saving faith? List the person or people who introduced you to Jesus or briefly describe how you came to know Him in saving faith.**

_____

_____

As we think about introducing people to Jesus Christ, we must realize that God is the One who accomplishes the work. We just get to be His instrument in the process. Jesus mentioned two principles that are involved in a person coming to faith.

1. God works to draw a person to faith in Jesus. Jesus said, "'No one can come to me unless the Father who sent me draws him'" (John 6:44).
2. People who are responsive to the Father come to Christ. Jesus said, "'Everyone who listens to the Father and learns from him comes to me'" (John 6:45).
   > ➧ **If the Holy Spirit will empower, enable, and give boldness to you, will you allow the Father to work through you so others can come to saving faith in Jesus Christ?**
   > ❑ Yes ❑ No Why or why not?_____

PARABLE OF THE WATER JUG

My dad grew up on a farm. One summer he went to help a neighbor plow his fields to prepare for planting his crops. It was a hot and humid day as he walked behind the mule team and the plow. Dripping with sweat he got very thirsty under the blazing summer sun. Dad took a break to get a drink of water.

The farmer spit out his tobacco juice and wiped his chin. Then he told my dad there was a water jug over under the tree in the shade. When my dad picked up the dusty glass jug, he could see green slime growing on the inside. With this sight of a dirty jug and thinking of the farmer's chewing tobacco, my dad decided he wasn't that thirsty and returned to his plowing.

As you pray and seek to reach out to those in your circles of influence, your life will be like a water jug. People who need Jesus Christ as Savior are thirsting for the Living Water. When they look at Christ through your "glass-jug" life, will they be thirsty enough to drink? Will they see the pure, clean Water of Life and decide to drink deeply. Or will they see impurities and uncleanness that cause them to put off a decision for Jesus Christ? How clean is your water jug?

> ➧ **If your life were like the water jug, how would you describe your jug? Check your response or write your own.**
> ❑ a. With Christ's help, I seek to keep my life clean and pure before God and man. I want Christ to show through my life.
> ❑ b. The outside may look clean to others, but I know what is on the inside. If people could see the inside, they would have second thoughts about taking a drink.

❑ c. I'm afraid my life would cause people to turn away from what I have to offer spiritually. They would probably decide they are not that thirsty.

❑ d. Other: _____

_____

➡ **Take a moment to pray. Ask God to help you experience His cleansing work so thoroughly in your life that people would be drawn to Jesus Christ and receive Him as the Living Water—as Savior.**

Pray also for your church and other Christians in your community that they, too, would be clean and not hinder people from coming to Jesus Christ.

Close your prayer with the prayer of the early church: "Lord... consider their threats and enable your servants to speak your word with great boldness" (Acts 4:29). Ask the Lord to prepare and empower you to introduce others to your Savior.

Optional Reading in *Concentric Circles of Concern*
1. A Premature Funeral, pages 179-180
2. A Crusade in Reno, pages 181-183

SOME WAYS TO INTRODUCE JESUS CHRIST

My dad pastored in Smithville, Tennessee. He offered a class on Sunday nights for several weeks to help the congregation know how to introduce others to Jesus Christ effectively. Each Sunday morning he would announce the study and ask everyone to participate.

Toward the end of the study, a man came to my dad after the morning service weeping. He drove an ambulance for the funeral home. He explained that he went out on a call the day before to a serious car accident. His best friend lay on the pavement dying. His friend said, "You go to church. Tell me how to be saved."

This church member wept as he confessed, "I didn't know what to tell him, and he died on the way to the hospital." Then he said, "Pastor, you need to teach us how to witness to people who need the Lord." My dad didn't have the heart to confront him with the fact that the class had been going on for weeks. This man just chose to ignore the opportunity. As a consequence, his best friend entered a godless eternity without Christ.

Don't wait too late to prepare yourself to tell others about your Savior. You probably will not meet them on their death bed. But the truth is: many of the people on your survey will enter a godless eternity without Christ unless *you* introduce them to your Savior. Let me suggest some ways to introduce Jesus Christ.

➥ **As you read the following suggestions, underline or draw a star beside the ones that appeal to you or those you have already used to introduce Jesus to others.**

1. Personal Testimony. If you have come to saving faith in Christ, you have a personal testimony. You can tell of the way you came to place your faith in Christ. You can testify to the difference life in Christ makes. You can tell about your personal relationship with Him. This is what a witness does. He describes his or her personal experience. Think through what you would say to (1) describe what life before Christ was like, (2) how you recognized your need for a Savior, (3) how you heard and responded to the gospel, and (4) what difference Jesus has made in your life (and be specific).

2. Gospel Tract or Book. A tract is a little leaflet or booklet that tells the gospel and what God has to say about salvation in the Bible. It usually guides the person to consider Christ's claims on his or her life. You can carry tracts in your pocket or purse to share with a person you may encounter during the day. You may just give the tract with a word of explanation and let the person read it in the privacy of his or her home. Better still, you can read through the tract with the person and answer questions he may have. This, coupled with your own testimony, can be an effective witness when God is already working to draw the person to Jesus. You should be able to get appropriate tracts at your church or a local Christian bookstore.

3. Marked New Testament. Christian bookstores have inexpensive New Testaments that have been prepared to use in sharing the gospel. They guide the reader to key verses of Scripture by directing them to the appropriate pages. Usually a footnote explains the Scripture and directs to the next verse. After reading the Scriptures, a person is invited to pray a prayer of repentance and faith in Christ. Like tracts, you can give the New Testament for private use or you can read through the plan of salvation with your friend.

I know a church in Oakland, California, that sought to minister in a very bad part of the community. Drugs, crime, violence, prostitution, gangs—they had it all. The pastor led the church to start praying for their community and learn how to share their faith. Someone donated 12,000 marked New Testaments with the title: "Here's Hope: Jesus Cares for You." One Saturday, many members gathered to distribute them door-to-door in the community.

When they presented the New Testament at the door, they received a common response, "If you know where I can find hope, you've got to tell me. Because I don't have any hope." In a single day they saw 659 people pray to receive Christ as Savior. When I talked to the pastor they had postponed their Spring "revival" services because they needed a bigger space for the services. God can use His Word to draw people to His Son.

4. Video, Movie, or Television Special. Today we are blessed with many quality presentations of the gospel through movies. *Jesus* is a video about the life of Christ using the gospel of Luke as the primary dialog. Millions of people worldwide have been introduced to Jesus through this film. You can secure this or another video to share with friends in your own home. Billy Graham and other evangelists have special crusades broadcast to present the gospel. Throw a party and invite your most wanted over for a movie. Let God use the media presentation to help introduce your friend to Jesus.

5. Church Bible Class and Worship. As I quoted earlier, Jesus said, "'Everyone who listens to the Father and learns from him comes to me'" (John 6:45). Invite your most wanted to join you for Sunday School class and/or worship at your church. Invite children to Vacation Bible School. As people sit under the teaching and preaching of God's Word, God's Holy Spirit can bring conviction of sin and draw them to the Savior. Stay in close relationship with them during this time. Be prepared to answer questions and show genuine interest in their spiritual well-being. Special presentations at Easter and Christmas may be ideal times to invite your most wanted to join you.

➥ **The methods described above should be very non-threatening for you as a witness and for the person you are sharing with. Which one(s), if any, do you think your most wanted person might respond to? Check any that apply.**
❑ 1. Personal Testimony
❑ 2. Gospel Tract or Book
❑ 3. Marked New Testament
❑ 4. Video or Movie
❑ 5. Church Bible Class and Worship

6. Memorized Plan of Salvation. Many churches, denomina-tions and parachurch groups offer courses where you can learn to share a detailed plan of salvation with others. They may use one of the methods I've already mentioned. Some help you memorize an outline and Scriptures to share the gospel. They help you under-stand how to answer common questions that people ask. This is usually coupled with on-the-job training with an experienced train-er. At first thought, this may seem too mechanical or "canned." However, once you have mastered the message you can share the essentials of the gospel in a very natural and appealing way.

In one church I served on staff, I coordinated the church's evan-gelism program for several semesters (after I had taken the course myself). We visited people who were newcomers to town and those who visited our worship services. We saw many people come to faith in Christ this way. However, by far the greater fruit came in a different way. Once people learned to share the gospel, they very naturally began sharing Jesus with family, relatives, friends, neigh-bors, and coworkers. Ask the Lord whether such a course is in His plan for your preparation. Then follow His leadership.

7. Outreach Bible Study. People who express an interest in learning more about Christ can be invited to an outreach Bible study. You can either use a prepared course of study or just guide a study of one of the gospels. The informality of a home or club-house at the apartment complex, reduces their fear of "church." A couple or team can host this study, cultivate relationships with participants, share their own life story, and answer questions of those who are seeking Christ. Many churches use this approach to start new "minichurches" (a small church within the church) as the people come to faith in Christ. I know of one church that has well over 100 groups meeting in apartments, homes, and other places outside the church building. Often a layperson serves as Bible teacher and pastor to the participants.

➡ **Do you know of places or people groups in your com-munity that God would have you target with an outreach Bible study? You wouldn't have to do it alone. A team from your church could do it together. Think about these possibilities. Check any for which God seems to impress you with a burden to reach.**

❑ apartment complex   ❑ assisted living facility
❑ neighborhood   ❑ government housing project
❑ jail or prison   ❑ nursing home
❑ college/university   ❑ Others? _____

8. Prayer Evangelism. Many Christians are finding that prayer for an unbeliever creates an openness to the gospel. For instance Youth With A Mission (YWAM) in Metro New York City use what they call a Prayer Station on the streets of the city. Intercessors wear a bright colored vest that says "Prayer Changes Things." People on each end of the block distribute flyers and invite people to stop by the Prayer Station to receive prayer for their felt needs. Many people are so broken and hurting they will ask you to pray for their needs. After prayer, the people often are open to hear the gospel or receive a tract or New Testament. When God answers the prayer, people have a living demonstration of His love and power.

Some people use prayer evangelism with their neighbors. Stop by your neighbor's house and tell them of your interest in praying for their felt needs. You might say something like, "I'm a Christian and I'm trying to take a greater interest in our neighborhood. I'm starting a prayer list so I can pray regularly for you and your family. Is there a special way I can pray for you today?" On the first visit you may catch them off guard. But pray for whatever they express as a need. Ask, "Would you mind if I pray right now?" Then pray. You may be surprised at the ways prayer will open doors and let you know how to reveal God's love by meeting needs as well. Follow up with a call, a visit, or have them over for dinner periodically.

9. "Canned Hunger." I heard about one church that used a variation of prayer evangelism in their neighborhoods. One week church members visit their neighbors and collect canned food for their local food bank. Most people will contribute something. Then say, "We want to thank you for participating in our food drive. Is there a way we can pray for you or your family in return?" Again pray for the expressed need and write it down so you can pray during the coming week.

The second week, church members go back to their neighbor's houses to report on the success of the food drive: *"We just wanted to let you know we collected _____ for the local food bank. We wanted to thank you again for participating."* Then give the person a gift of some kind (a tract, New Testament, *Jesus* Video, or something else that might have a gospel message in it). Say, *"I've been praying for _____ this week. Is there anything else I can pray for you?"* Watch for those who may be particular needy or responsive to let you know where the Father is at work. Then join Him.

➥ **The last four methods require more active participation, but they also can be the most rewarding as you experience a person being born again. As you read these methods, which one(s), if any, do you sense God may be leading you to participate in? Check any that apply.**
❏ 6. Memorized Plan of Salvation
❏ 7. Outreach Bible Study
❏ 8. Prayer Evangelism
❏ 9. "Canned Hunger"

10. A Divine Network. I met a doctor in Florida who had a very busy family practice. He wanted to be a man of integrity with his office schedule, but he also wanted to take an interest in his patient's spiritual condition also. First, he prepared a faith history that was taken at the same time as the medical history. The nurse would just explain, "Research shows that faith has an influence on health and healing. I'd like to ask you a few questions about your faith history." Simple questions about such things as worship attendance, prayer, and Bible reading would give Walt an idea of their openness to spiritual matters.

Walt said he didn't have time to share the gospel with his patients and stay on schedule, though he often prayed with those who were open to his doing so. When he diagnosed a man with prostate cancer, he would sit him down and tell him the bad news. Then he would write a prescription that had Bob's name and phone number on it. He said, "Bob is a wonderful friend of mine. He has been through everything you are about to go through. You give him a call and he will explain some of the things you'll be facing. He will even come by the hospital when we do your surgery. Best of all: He's free."

I call this Walt's divine network. Bob and others with different gifts and experiences are members of Walt's church. One lady ministers to new mothers who want to breast feed their baby. They are gifted at showing mercy and love. They also are gifted at introducing people to Jesus Christ. Walt networks these Christians with his patients who need to know the Lord and who have a special need. As these coworkers with Christ show love and meet needs, they also have a chance to lead the person to faith in Christ.

Though you may not be a doctor, you have a divine network. It is called the Body of Christ. Begin to pray and ask the Lord how He wants to network you together with others to see people come to faith in Christ. You may be the one who needs to link up with a person gifted at prayer or evangelism. On the other hand, you may be the one who is gifted and needs to be linked to other members of the Body of Christ.

Your Divine Network

In *Concentric Circles of Concern*, Oscar Thompson tells the story of a couple named Alice and John. Alice was a Christian and church member, but John was not a Christian. Oscar had a group of men he called his S.W.A.T. Team (Spiritual Weapons and Tactics). This group targeted John. They prayed for him. Took him to lunch. Played tennis with him. He began attending church with his wife. Over a period of time under the preaching of God's Word and experiencing a loving group of men, John came to a radical and personal faith in Christ.

Every church needs some S.W.A.T. teams by whatever name you call them. We need to be intentional in reaching out to others for the cause of Christ. In some cases this will be a team of people who sense God's special calling to the target group. In other cases this team may be an existing group that gives part of their attention to outreach and witness. Here are some names you might choose from, but you may be very creative in naming your groups.

➡ **Which of the following names seem more appealing to you as a title for an outreach team? Check any that apply or list some thoughts of your own.**
❑ Divine Network
❑ S.W.A.T. team (Spiritual Weapons and Tactics)
❑ Outreach Team
❑ Task Force
❑ Impact Group
❑ Care Group
❑ Evangelism Team
❑ Sunday School Class (yes they can be a team)
❑ Cell Group
❑ Minichurch
❑ Others: _____

You may be the one who needs a network to help you. Like Walt (the doctor) you may need some people who would feel called to network with you at work, in your neighborhood, or with some of the people on your most wanted list.

➥ **If God were to call them out, what kind of people would you like to network with to help you obey the final command? Check any that apply.**
  ❑ a prayer warrior/intercessor who will pray specifically for me and my most wanted
  ❑ someone who is gifted at building relationships and showing God's love (like the S.W.A.T. team that reached out to John)
  ❑ someone who is gifted at sharing the plan of salvation and leading a person to personal faith in Christ
  ❑ someone who will partner with me in outreach by visiting together, praying together, or working in an outreach project together
  ❑ someone who can help a new believer grow in his faith and discipleship

➥ **Before you begin this next activity, pray. Ask God to give you a special burden or insight into what He wants to do in your church or through your life. If possible, work through this activity with a group of people or with your whole church. Ask God to begin networking you together to reach people for Christ.**

➥ **Read through the following list of suggestions for specialized outreach groups. Write a plus sign (+) by any one or more that you sense a deep need for in your church. Check any that you sense God may be calling you to participate in. Add any others that may come to mind that are not in this list. A team to reach...**
  ❑ husbands who need the Lord
  ❑ wives who need the Lord
  ❑ wayward children who need the Lord
  ❑ parents of Christian youth
  ❑ apartment dwellers (in many places 90% are unchurched)
  ❑ youth and older children
  ❑ college and university students
  ❑ international students
  ❑ single parents
  ❑ divorced individuals
  ❑ senior adults
  ❑ people in nursing homes or assisted living facilities
  ❑ athletes
  ❑ business executives/owners

- ❑ deaf people
- ❑ drug addicts, alcoholics
- ❑ families with invalid or disabled children or adults
- ❑ homeless people
- ❑ immigrants from different ethnic background
- ❑ inmates and prisoners in jail or prison
- ❑ international workers temporarily in your area
- ❑ migrant workers
- ❑ newlyweds
- ❑ prostitutes
- ❑ retirees
- ❑ doctors, nurses, other health care professionals
- ❑ school teachers and administrators
- ❑ some other specialized group of workers
- ❑ tourists who visit our town/local events/attractions
- ❑ unemployed people
- ❑ workers at major employers
- ❑ workers at your place of employment
- ❑ young married couples
- ❑ people who visit your church who need Christ
- ❑ Others: ________________________________

____

____

____

____

____

Work together with others in your church or even together with other churches in your city to be intentional in obeying the final command. Remember God's will is that none perish but all come to repentance. Pray together. Share burdens, needs, ideas, and testimonies. Ask the Lord to teach you how He wants to reach the group(s) that you have targeted.

➥ **If you are working through this book alone, write below the name of one or more people that might become partners with you in obeying the final command. If you are working through this with a group, list below the names and contact information of those who share a common interest, burden, or calling.**

____

____

____

____

6. Teach New Believers to Obey

> "'Go and make disciples of all nations... <u>teaching them to obey everything</u> I have commanded you'" (Matt. 28:19-20).

Part of the final command of the Lord is to teach disciples to obey everything He has commanded them. This is an assignment for the Body of Christ. A person does not learn to be a well rounded and mature disciple apart from the rest of the Body. Together with the Body of Christ you need to model complete obedience. You need to do your part in teaching obedience to others.

➡ **How were you taught to obey all the commands of Christ. Check your response or write your own.**

❑ a. A teacher or mentor used a very thorough process of teaching me Christ's commands and helping me develop healthy spiritual disciplines in my life.

❑ in a group ❑ one-on-one

❑ b. I have studied a variety of courses that have helped me develop my obedience.

❑ c. I went to Bible College and/or seminary to study.

❑ d. I was just expected to pick it up from Sunday School and/or preaching services.

❑ e. I read and studied the Bible on my own and prayed for the Holy Spirit to guide me.

❑ f. I didn't even know that Christ commanded complete obedience.

❑ g. Other: _____

_____

If you are like many people these days, you probably had to respond by checking d, e, or f. Too often, new believers are left to figure out the Christian life slowly and on their own. They go to church but no one takes time to explain the basics. Consequently, many Christians are living a very weak and ineffective life. Obedience to the final command is not complete until we have made <u>disciples not just decisions</u>.

➤ **If God were to grade you today on your level of obedience to all His commands, what grade do you think He would give you? Check one.**

❑ A—Your obedience is about as close to complete as a human being can live.

❑ B—You know the commands and seek to keep them most of the time, but you still have a few areas where you fail to obey as you should.

❑ C—You want to be obedient and do your best, but you really don't know God's commands very well. Consequently you fail to obey in areas you are not even aware of.

❑ D—You consistently fail in many ways in living up to God's standards described in His Word.

❑ F—You don't know the commands and make no effort to obey. From God's perspective you are about like those who are lost.

An activity like that can be pretty convicting. If you haven't had a proper foundation for being taught to obey, more than likely, your obedience is lacking. If you haven't already done so, I want you and your church to begin taking this part of the final command seriously.

The Value of Group Discipleship Training

Paul instructed Timothy: "The things you have heard me say in the presence of many witnesses entrust to reliable men who will also be qualified to teach others" (2 Tim. 2:2). Paul taught Timothy to be a disciple in the presence of others (this was a group discipling process). He probably taught him one-on-one at other times. Paul knew about the importance of the Body of Christ and how it needs the ministry of all the parts to be the healthiest possible Body of Christ.

God has placed us in the Body of Christ because we need each other, and we benefit from our togetherness. We can help each other be the best disciples we can be:

> "Let us consider how we may spur one another
> on toward love and good deeds. Let us not give up
> meeting together, as some are in the habit of doing,
> but let us encourage one another—and all the more
> as you see the Day approaching" (Heb. 10:24-25).

The value of discipleship training in a small group is that we can benefit from the ideas, encouragement, examples, insights, testimonies, prayers, and accountability that come from others. These small groups do not get together just for Bible study—though the Bible must be treated as the primary text book. The group needs to be a healthy and functioning Body of Christ in miniature. I call it a minichurch (a small church within the church).

When you approach the Bible as your Guide, you will probably take one of three approaches:

1. The Human Centered Approach. This was the approach of the Sadducees. Jesus said to them: "You do not know the Scriptures or the power of God" (Mark 12:24). They relied on their own wisdom and human reasoning to determine God's will and purposes. They ignored what God had said and what He could do.

2. The Bible Centered Approach. This was the approach of the Pharisees and Jewish leaders. Jesus said to them: "You diligently study the Scriptures because you think that by them you possess eternal life.... yet you refuse to come to me to have life" (John 5:39-40). Bible knowledge and even Bible mastery is not what God is looking for. That is only a means to an end—a personal love relationship with Jesus Christ. These Bible students stopped short of the real thing.

3. The Christ Centered Approach. In the same passage Jesus said, "These are the Scriptures that testify about me...come to me to have life" (John 5:39-40). Bible study should point us to the relationship with Christ. When we come to Him He gives us real life, abundant life.

➥ **Which approach do you and your church use most frequently in your use of the Bible as a guide? Check one.**

 ❏ a. The Human Centered Approach. We don't use the Bible much, don't know it, and seldom see or experience God's power.

 ❏ b. The Bible Centered Approach. We study the Bible diligently, but we've settled for the head knowledge and have little experience of the presence and power of Christ in our lives.

 ❏ c. The Christ Centered Approach. We study and use the Bible, but we go on to the relationship to Christ and the application of His Word in our lives. We have tasted of the abundant life in His presence and with His power.

As you teach new believers to become disciples, you must use the Bible as your primary textbook. But you must help them move beyond a head knowledge to an experience of a genuine and intimate relationship with Christ. The following suggestions are areas we need to teach new believers and help them obey. I've addressed some of these areas in discipleship courses I've developed to help you study the Scriptures and move to a relationship to Christ. I've pointed you to those resources where appropriate.

* Help new believers learn to pray effectively in their private prayer life and together with other believers in corporate prayer. (See *In God's Presence*, p. 111.)
* Introduce new believers to the Bible and teach them how to study it, meditate on it, use it as a guide, and then apply it to daily living.
* Help new believers establish an intimate love relationship with Christ, and help them understand how to know and do His will. (See *Experiencing God*, p. 110.)
* Teach new believers the proper foundations and disciplines for life in Christ and how to learn from Christ to be Christlike. (See *The Mind of Christ*, p. 111.)
* Guide new believers to survey their world and obey the final command. Help them introduce their world to Jesus.
* Teach new believers their relationship to the Body of Christ and help them become intimately involved with a small group (or minichurch) for fellowship, growth, support, and ministry to others. (See *Interacting with God in Ephesians*, p. 112)

➥ **What are some of the ways your church already helps teach new believers to obey. Check all that apply. If you don't know, do some research to find out.**

❑ sermons and worship services
❑ assign a one-on-one new Christian encourager/mentor
❑ new Christian's class
❑ Bible study classes like Church or Sunday School
❑ small-group "body life" experiences like a cell group, care group, fellowship group, or minichurch
❑ in-depth discipleship training courses
❑ seminars and workshops
❑ study *Survival Kit for New Christians*
❑ media library with print, audio, and video resources
❑ pastor's class for new Christians
❑ information and opportunities to attend conferences
Others: _____

_____

_____

_____

➥ Think about your own discipleship training. What do you sense is your greatest need at the present time? Is there something specific you sense you need to participate in to meet that need?

_____

_____

_____

➥ What could your church do to help you do a better job in your own obedience? Check any that apply or add your own.
   ❑ provide small-group or minichurch for fellowship, encouragement, and help from the Body of Christ
   ❑ provide in-depth discipleship courses
   ❑ offer seminars, workshops, or conferences
   ❑ provide print, video, and audio resources for personal use
   ❑ pair me up with a mentor or partner for accountability
   Others: _____

   _____

   _____

ADDITIONAL HELPS—BOOK UPDATES
Go to www.FinalCommand.com and check "Book Updates" for additional information, suggestions, resources, vendors and world wide web links.

Teach New Believers to Obey the FINAL COMMAND

When a person first comes to faith in Christ, he probably has more non-Christian family and friends than will ever be true again. Too often we have encouraged people to stay away from their old friends. Let's take a different approach and work together with new believers to see their family and friends come to Christ. Instead of reaching one person, we can reach a family or group.

When you reach people for faith in Christ, begin to help them work through this *Final Command Action Manual*. This very process will help them take their growth in Christ seriously, because the salvation of their closest relatives and friends depends on it. Helping them with this process will also insure that you are nearby to "teach them to obey everything."

- Help them immediately begin listing the people in their circles of influence on the survey sheets.
- Pray with them to determine the people in their family, friends, or coworkers that most need Christ.
- Help them examine the ways God may indicated the people who are most ready and will be most responsive as the "most wanted."
- Pray with them for their most wanted. In the process you'll be training them in the art of intercession.
- Help them reconcile broken relationships—first with God and then with others. This very process of reconciling relationships as a new believer may be the most convincing proof to others that his or her salvation is genuine.
- Help them introduce their most wanted to Jesus Christ through their own personal testimonies. You may walk with them into their world and be a help in sharing the gospel more thoroughly.
- Don't quit until you have seen this new believer's world come to faith in Christ.

➡ **Now that you've experienced at least the message of this action manual, think about the people in your church or the Christians in your circles of influence. Is there a person you already know that would benefit from your help in "obeying the final command"? Or is there a person you would like to partner with so that you both can help each other obey the final command? If you think of a person (or persons), write his or her name below.**

_____

➡ **Now the more important question: Would you be willing to help that person obey the final command so his or her world can come to faith in Christ. Will you make the contact and give the invitation to help?**
❏ Yes ❏ No ❏ Yes, but not yet.

➡ **Now pause to pray. Ask the Lord to:**
- help you obey all that He has commanded you.
- reveal to you the areas where you are lacking in obedience, so that you can obey.
- help your church to teach all believers to be obedient disciples.
- reveal your role in the Body of Christ teaching obedience.

7. Go to the Ends of the Earth

When Jesus issued the final command, He did not leave out any objects of His love. He commanded us to make disciples of "<u>all</u> nations" or all peoples and ethnic groups. In Mark 16:15 He said, "Go into <u>all</u> the world and preach the gospel to <u>every</u> creature." Then in Acts, just before He ascended into heaven, He said:

> "'You will receive power when the Holy Spirit comes on you; and you will be my witnesses in Jerusalem, and in all Judea and Samaria, and to the ends of the earth'" (Acts 1:8).

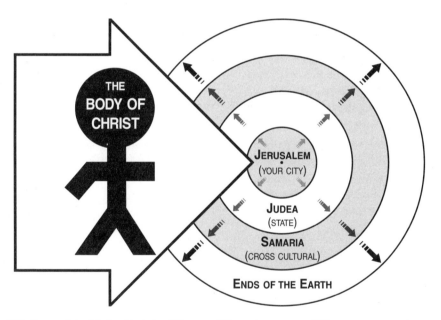

We have his Holy Spirit. We are His witnesses. We must start in...
- Jerusalem (at home, in your city),
- continue into Judea (extended family, surrounding communities, county, state, or province),
- then to Samaria (crossing racial, ethnic, and religious barriers),
- and continue to the ends of the earth.

The whole world is the object of the final command. "The Lord is... longsuffering toward us, not willing that any should perish but that <u>all</u> should come to repentance" (2 Pet. 3:9). We are to carry the gospel to ALL peoples of ALL the world. What a humanly impossible assignment! Fortunately, God is with us always to empower us by His Spirit to carry out the assignment. But we must choose to obey Him. He does not have an alternate plan if we refuse His command.

Jesus didn't issue the final command to an elite corps of super disciples. He gave the command to a group of ordinary men and to all who would come to faith through their message—that includes you and me. Collectively, we are the Body of Christ for our generation. Every Christian and every local congregation of Christians are parts of that larger Body of Christ. Every part is needed for the whole body to function as Christ intended. If the whole church (every individual believer in a local congregation and every congregation throughout the world) would obey the final command, God would see to it that the whole world would hear the good news about His Son. With God all things are possible. His plan is this:

> ## The Whole Body of Christ
> ## Reaching the Whole World with the Gospel

Since the command was given to so many, you might be tempted to think your part is so small that it doesn't matter. Let's look at an important parable of Jesus. During the days before the cross, Jesus gave many significant messages to His disciples. He told the parable of the talents, recorded in Matthew 25:14-30.

THE PARABLE OF THE TALENTS

A master was going on a long journey (just as Jesus was going to heaven). The master entrusted his property to His servants so they could carry on his work in his absence (just as Jesus entrusts us with His Spirit and His gifts to do His work). The master gave one servant five talents (money not skills). To a second servant he gave two talents of money, and to a third he gave only one talent. In a similar way, God gives us His Holy Spirit and a variety of gifts (special manifestations of the Holy Spirit for the carrying out of God's work). Some of God's servants have multiple and powerful gifts.

Others have fewer gifts, but the Scripture says, "to <u>each one</u> the manifestation of the Spirit is given for the common good... and he gives them to <u>each one</u> just as he determines" (1 Cor. 12:7, 11).

➥ **As you look at your own life, would you say you are one of the more gifted servants in Christ's kingdom or one of the lesser gifted servants? Check one.**

❑ a. I'm a "five-talent servant." I'm humbled by the privilege and awed at the great responsibility.

❑ b. I'm probably a "two-talent servant." I am gifted but not with the great variety I observe in others.

❑ c. I'm only a "one-talent servant." I'm not even sure what my gift might be. The gift I have doesn't look like much compared to others.

In every church there are some "five-talent servants." Perhaps your pastor, staff, and some other key leaders would be these very gifted servants. There are also some "two-talent servants." There are more of these, but they are all important to the function of the Body. Then there are many "one-talent servants." Probably, most people who complete this exercise would check "c." Were you one of these?

After a long time, the master of the servants returned (just as Jesus will one day return at His second coming). The master asked for an accounting for what was done with his property (just as each one of us will give an accounting to God, Romans 14:12). The servant with five talents had earned five more, and the servant with two talents had earned two more. The servant with one talent was afraid, and so he had hidden the talent rather than use it. He had nothing but the unused talent to return to the master.

➥ **Based on the fruitfulness of your spiritual life, in which of these two categories do you find yourself? Check one.**

❑ a. I'm using the gifts God has given me, and God is producing fruit through my life to His glory.

❑ b. I'm not using my gift(s). I don't have much (or any) fruitfulness to show.

In most churches I know the vast majority of people, if they are truthful, would have to confess that "b" is the truth about their spiritual life. For a variety of reasons, most who claim the name Christian do not get involved in serving their Master. Most are content to be spectators at worship, in Bible class, or in the service and ministry of the Body of Christ.

The master in the parable made a judgment about the quality of the service rendered by the servants. The first two servants used their talents and had increased the master's property. Both these servants were commended in the same way even though one had gained more to return. The master said to both: "Well done, good and faithful servant! You have been faithful with a few things; I will put you in charge of many things. Come and share your master's happiness!" (Matt. 25:21). I don't know about you, but I surely would like to get that kind of commendation!

The servant with one unused talent is a different story. To this servant the master replied, "You wicked, lazy servant!... Take the talent from him and give it to the one who has the ten talents.... And throw that worthless servant outside, into the darkness, where there will be weeping and gnashing of teeth" (Matt. 25:26, 28, 30). Again, I don't know about you, but I surely would NOT want to receive that judgment.

➡ **Based upon the way you use your spiritual gifts, which kind of response can you expect from your Master. Check one.**

❑ a. I am actively using what gifts I have for the Lord, and He is producing fruit. I can anticipate being commended as a faithful servant.

❑ b. I haven't been using my gift(s) at all. I don't have any fruit to show. All I can expect is a severe rebuke from the Lord.

Did you notice in the parable that the <u>most gifted</u> servants were not the ones who got in trouble with the master? It was the <u>least gifted</u> servant that got in trouble, because he didn't use what he had for the master's benefit. I'm afraid that in most of our churches, the large number of "least gifted" servants are headed for severe rebuke and judgment for refusing to use their gift(s) for the Master. We're not talking about mere money like the parable. The gift of eternal life, the gift of the Holy Spirit, and the gifts of His Spirit for service were not purchased with money. No, they were purchased with Jesus' broken body, shed blood, and His very life laid down for you on the cross. Paul said for this reason:

"<u>Christ's love compels us</u>, because we are convinced that one died for all, and therefore all died. And he died for all, that <u>those who live should no longer live for themselves but for him who died for them</u> and was raised again" (2 Cor. 5:14-15).

My dear brothers and sisters in Christ, it's not too late! Christ's love ought to compel you to live in active service for Him. Don't be a "wicked, lazy servant" any longer. **If no one else obeys the final command, you choose this day to be the one who does!**

Dear churches (the Body of Christ), do you love your brothers and sisters in Christ? Jesus said the way we love one another will be the clear evidence that we are His disciples (John 13:35). John emphasized in 1 John that the way we love our brothers is a clear demonstration of how much we love God. Based upon the truth of the Parable of the Talents, if we love our brothers and sisters, we WILL NOT allow the least gifted among us to hide their "talent" any longer. Knowing the kind of judgment that will bring, knowing the blessing of the Master's happiness that will be missed, knowing the loss this causes for the kingdom, knowing that the very life and eternal destiny of the people of the world depends upon the response, and knowing the "weeping and gnashing of teeth" that awaits, we will make every effort to "spur one another on toward love and good deeds." (Heb. 10:25). In the very next verse, the writer of Hebrews continues with a sober warning. Read it carefully.

> If we deliberately keep on sinning after we have received the knowledge of the truth, no sacrifice for sins is left, but only a fearful expectation of judgment and of raging fire that will consume the enemies of God. Anyone who rejected the law of Moses died without mercy on the testimony of two or three witnesses. How much more severely do you think a man deserves to be punished who has trampled the Son of God under foot, who has treated as an unholy thing the blood of the covenant that sanctified him, and who has insulted the Spirit of grace? For we know him who said, "It is mine to avenge; I will repay," and again, "The Lord will judge his people." It is a dreadful thing to fall into the hands of the living God (Heb. 10:26-31).

If we are ever to take the commands of the Lord seriously, we must take the final command seriously! The Lord's return from His long journey is close at hand—He could return at any time. We can't wait. We can't continue to say, "the harvest is four months away." We can't continue to permit our brothers and sisters to live in jeopardy by hiding and not using their gifts. We must mobilize the WHOLE church for the harvest. We must carry this gospel of Jesus Christ to the ends of the earth!

➥ **What is God saying to you right now? What do you sense He is calling you to do in response to this message? I don't want to guess for you. Reflect on what the Holy Spirit is saying and write a summary of what you sense He is saying to you and to your church.**

The final command extends to the ends of the earth. Henry Blackaby says it this way, "Every local church is a <u>world</u> missions strategy center." You and your church need to be thinking, planning, and actively taking the gospel to your immediate world AND to the ends of the earth. Already, I've been guiding you to prepare for and to share the gospel with your immediate world— those in your circles of influence on your survey. Now I want to turn your focus to the ends of the earth. I'll help you begin thinking of the ways God has and may call you and your church to participate in taking the gospel to "Judea and Samaria, and to the ends of the earth."

Missions Awareness

One place to begin is by becoming aware of God's work in other areas. I am going to use the term *missions* God's work through the Body of Christ to reach a lost world with the gospel of Jesus Christ. This could include "home missions" (in your country) and "international missions" (in other countries of the world). When you begin to learn about missions, God may guide you in specific ways to be involved through your support or personal involvement.

➥ **Read the following suggestions for developing missions awareness. Circle one or more that you are willing to do to increase your awareness of God's work in the world.**
   1. Read a biography. Many missionaries say they first sensed God's call to missions while reading a biography of a missionary. (e.g. William Carey, Adoniram Judson, David Brainerd, John "Praying" Hyde, David

Livingstone, Jim Elliott, Hudson Tailor, Bertha Smith, Amy Carmichael, William Booth, C. T. Studd, etc.)

2. Read about the history of missions of a missions group, a denomination, a parachurch group, of a people group, or a country.
3. Watch a video or documentary that tells the story of a missionary or a particular mission effort.
4. Read or listen to news reports and updates from the missions field. This may come from missions magazines, Christian radio, Christian television, newsletters from missionaries, e-mail groups, and Internet web sites.
5. Attend a missions conference where missionaries give live reports about their work.
6. Listen to the testimonies of those who have been touched by missions efforts.

➡ **What will you do to increase your missions awareness?**

_____

_____

Missions Support

Missions awareness is not obedience to the final command. It just prepares you and helps you hear what God may want to do through you. As you become aware of God's activity in a missions area, you can begin to identify ways He is inviting you to join Him in missions support or involvement. Missions support occurs when you provide help to others who are involved in missions work. This is a beginning of obedience to the final command. Just as Paul received support from churches in the area of finances, persons to help, and through prayers, missionaries need support.

➡ **Read the following suggestions for participating in missions support. Circle one or more that you are willing to do to provide support for missions work outside your local church.**

1. Praying for missions and missionaries. Pray for:
   • a missionary, his or her family and work
   • missionaries on their birthdays
   • specific requests given by missionaries or organizations
   • missions organization, administrators, staff
   • gateway cities, countries, and areas where missionaries serve

- unreached people group (your church can even "adopt" a people group
- God to call people to missions involvement
- conversion of people in a non-Christian religion (groups pray for Moslems during Ramadan, Jews, Hindus, Buddhists, etc.)
- governments and leaders whose laws may grant freedom or hinder missions work in a country
- national leaders (Christian workers in their own country or culture)
- missions events, crusades, or outreach efforts
- use of media like the *Jesus* film or Gideon Bibles to reach people for Christ

2. Encouragement: write letters, send e-mail, send personal gifts, call, etc. to encourage missionaries in their work. Be careful, however, not to do so in a way that would become a hindrance because of the amount of time involved.

3. Financial Support. Obey the Lord's directions in giving money to:
   - your church for missions causes
   - individual missionaries and their projects
   - missionary sending organizations
   - schools that train and equip missionaries for service
   - emergency requests for disaster relief or hunger projects
   - individuals who are going on short- or long-term mission trips
   - Bible societies, missions radio and television
   - churches or organizations that support national pastors and missionaries in other countries

4. Material Support. You may have material you can give either from your personal property or your company (e.g. medical supplies, food for disaster relief, clothes, blankets, bicycles, cars, Christian books or literature, Bibles, radio or video equipment, etc.) Don't send material without knowledge of a specific need.

5. Logistical Support. Your work or company may be able to provide logistical help for missionaries. Coordinate travel, shipment of goods, transfer of data, technical training, etc.

6. Your children. Parents and grandparents are sometimes the greatest hindrance to individuals who sense God's

call to missions. If your children or grandchildren feel called to missions, give them your blessing. Send them off with your encouragement. Provide all the above kinds of support at your disposal. Your greatest contribution to the final command could come through Godly children who respond to God's call.

➡ **What will you do to obey the final command by supporting missions at home and abroad?**

_____
_____
_____
_____
_____
_____

Missions Involvement

You can obey the final command by getting involved in missions and actually taking the gospel to the ends of the earth in person. Nearly anyone, everyone, can become involved in missions. You don't have to be a career missionary to get involved in person.

➡ **Read the following suggestions for missions involvement. Circle one or more that you are willing to do to be involved in missions work outside your local church.**

1. Go as a volunteer on a short-term missions trip.
   - evangelism project
   - Bible distribution
   - construction project
   - medical/dental clinics
   - discipleship training for people and churches
   - ministry to missionary children while their parents are involved in meetings or events
   - music, dramatic presentations (individual or group)
   - health projects (e.g. drilling water wells, building ponds/reservoir)
   - disaster relief effort (hurricane, earthquake, famine, etc.)
   - prayerwalking (praying "on site with insight") particularly in countries with limited access for missionaries
   - feeding projects
   - teaching (e.g. English as a Second Language)
   - ministry to orphans, lepers
   - agricultural project
   - sports clinic, demonstrations

2. Minister to people in your area who could carry the gospel home with them.
   - international students at the university
   - foreign exchange students
   - international tourists at local attractions
   - international athletes in training or at sporting events
   - employees who are only working in your area on a temporary basis and will be returning to their home country
3. If God should call you, go as a career or long-term missionary in one of the following ways (or others God may reveal)
   - through your denomination's sending agency
   - sponsored by your church or a group of churches
   - tentmaking (you provide you own income through employment and serve in missions as a "volunteer")
   - parachurch group assignment (you normally raise your own support before going and periodically as the need arises)

➥ **What will you do to obey the final command by personal involvement in going and participating in missions? I want you to be involved in missions, but remember God is your Master. He calls to missions involvement. What do you presently sense God may be calling you to do?**

_____

_____

_____

_____

➥ **Close by taking time to pray. Surrender your life to be available to God for whatever He asks and where ever He leads. Consider David Livingstone's prayer as your own.**

Lord, send me anywhere, only go with me.
Lay any burden on me, only sustain me.
Sever any tie but the tie that binds me to Thyself.

LEADER'S GUIDE

Final Command Action Manual is designed so it can stand alone as an individual study. An individual can work through the book at his or her own pace. However, you will experience greater value by studying this resource together with other Christians. We need to repent of our disobedience and help every Christian find his or her place in the harvest. I recommend that you guide your entire church (youth and adults) through this study together. Better yet, work with other churches in your city to join God in making disciples of all the people in your city. You can use one of the methods described on pages 11-12.

• workshop (4-5 hours)
• short-term study (4 or 5 weekly sessions of an hour each.)
• supplement to your group's ongoing study (15-20 minutes each week for sharing, praying, and networking for obedience to the final command)
• retreat

BEFORE THE STUDY

You and your group or church need to prepare for use of this action manual. Complete the following actions to prepare yourself.

❏ 1. Read pages 6-26 and determine how you will use this book.
❏ 2. For best results, read *Concentric Circles of Concern* or at least read the "Optional Reading" assignments from *Concentric Circles of Concern* mentioned throughout this book in shaded boxes. Be prepared to share illustrations in your own words where appropriate
❏ 3. Whether you only have a few participants or a room full, plan on guiding the study in such a way that members will be able to share, discuss, and pray together in small groups of no more than eight to ten members. You, your pastor, or another leader can guide the larger group and then break down into the smaller groups for processing and applying the message.
❏ 4. Read through this "Leader's Guide" and determine which discussion questions and activities will be best for your group and your use plan. The following small group study suggestions follow the order of the book content. You can adapt them, divide them, combine them, or make other adjustments to best meet the needs of your group.

Spiritual Preparations

On the night before the cross, Jesus explained to His disciples that those who love Him will obey Him (John 14:15). The fact that the vast majority of Christians are not faithfully obeying the final command is an indicator that we do not love Him as we should. The very best way to help your people obey the final command is to help them return to their first love relationship with Jesus Christ. The Lord's Supper or Communion can be a sacred assembly of worship that reminds us of the great sacrifice of the Lord in such a way that we are restored to intimate fellowship with Him. Though it is not required, I'd like to recommend that your church or group work through *Come to the Lord's Table* (p. 109) as spiritual preparation for the use of the *Final Command Action Manual.* This three-week study may help restore or develop the foundation areas mentioned on pages 14-15. The more you can do to help prepare your people with a heart to obey the Lord, the more fruitful this study of the Final Command will be.

Order or Secure Resources

❑ *Final Command Action Manual.* Order one book for each member or participant from www.FinalCommand.com you can print out an order form for mailing if you prefer. Please allow up to three weeks for delivery.

❑ *Concentric Circles of Concern.* This book is optional but will be very helpful and inspirational for the leader. Order one copy for the large group leader or for each small group leader.

❑ Optional: *The Harvest* video (© 1998 by Venture Media). This video is a 17-minute parable that will stir the hearts of Christians to grasp the importance of all God's people being involved in bringing in the spiritual harvest. For additional details visit the web site at www.theharvest.com. To order go to www.goccc.com or call 1-800-352-8273. See page 26 for group activity suggestions.

Introducing Jesus Resources. Secure samples of resources for display during the study of Action 5: Introduce Jesus Christ. Many of these will be available from your church or consult with your pastor for other recommended resources. Check with your Christian bookstore or Christian Internet web sites like www.crosswalk.com/resources (evangelism). Include:

❑ gospel tracts like "Steps to Peace with God," "Eternal Life," or "4 Spiritual Laws"

❑ evangelistic books like *The Way to God* by Dwight L. Moody or *More Than a Carpenter* by Josh McDowell

❑ marked New Testament like *Here's Hope: Jesus Cares for You* (www.lifewaystores.com or 1-800-448-8032)

❑ movie like *Jesus* (from www.jesusvideo.org or 1-888-537-8736) or a Billy Graham film like *The Ride* or *A Vow to Cherish* (from World Wide Pictures at www.shop.wwp.org or 1-800-501-4557) Note that most videos are licensed only for private home use and not public or church viewing.

❑ In-depth evangelism training curriculum like *Evangelism Explosion* (www.eeinternational.org or 954-491-6100)

Visual Aids. Secure visual aids to assist learning:

❑ An 8-10" piece of PVC pipe for the parable on page 51.

❑ A clear glass jug (dirty is okay) for the parable on page 72.

❑ *Missions Awareness and Involvement.* Secure materials from your church or denomination that identify ways people can be involved in missions awareness, short-term missions involvement, and career missions opportunities. Include sample biographies from the list on pages 93-94 that members can either purchase or check out for reading. For web sites look for missions links at www.crosswalk.com or one prepared by your denominational missions sending agency.

❑ *Discipleship Training.* Secure samples of curriculum used in your church, recommended resources for equipping members in Christian discipleship, or information about training opportunities already available in your church.

ADDITIONAL HELPS—BOOK UPDATES
Go to www.FinalCommand.com and check "Book Updates" for additional information, suggestions, resources, vendors and world wide web links.

SMALL GROUP STUDY SUGGESTIONS

Use the following suggestions for reading, discussing, and applying the seven actions for obedience to the final command. You can ask members to turn to these pages and identify the questions or activities you want them to share or discuss in their small groups. Combine or divide the sections according to the number of sessions you have planned and the time available.

"Seven Stages..." and "Introductions" (pp. 6-17)

1. How is *Final Command Action Manual* going to be different than just reading through a book? (p. 9)
2. Briefly describe in your own words the five foundations for a healthy and fruitful Body of Christ (pp. 14-15). What others, if any, would you add to these five?
3. Which of these foundations do you think contributes most to reaching a lost world for Christ and why?
4. In which of these foundation areas is our church the weakest? How do you think that affects our reaching the lost for faith in Christ? What do you sense we need to do to grow stronger in this area?
5. Briefly describe in your own words the seven actions for obedience to the final command.
6. Based on these brief summaries, which of these actions will you be most interested in studying and applying and why?

"Jesus' Final Command" (pp. 18-22)

1. What level of importance do you think Jesus placed on this final command with His disciples?
2. Volunteers: share your responses to the activity on page 20.
3. How well do you think the majority of members in our church are doing in obedience to the final command? What evidence would you offer to support your opinion?
4. If you (and/or your church) have confessed to disobedience to the final command, pray the prayer of repentance (p. 21) or spend time for members to verbalize their own prayers to the Lord.
5. Share your responses to the activities on page 22. What are some ways we can encourage others in our church to join in obedience to the final command. Enter into a covenant (pp. 106-108) with each other to help each other obey the final command.

"The Harvest Is Ready" (pp. 23-26)

1. If Jesus were to examine our lives and our church, would He conclude that we are serious about the ripe harvest or that we have put it off until later? Why? What evidence is there?
2. In the past, have you seen the harvest as something everyone should have a part in or as something only a gifted few participate in? Why?
3. What are some of the ways the members in the Arkansas church (p. 24) cooperated in reaching this family for Christ?

4. What difference do you think we would make in our community, if every member found a place to be involved in the harvest?
5. Read Luke 10:2-3. Pray for the Lord to call workers into the harvest field. Ask God to call each of us to our places in the harvest.
6. Watch *The Harvest* video and complete the activities on page 26.

Actions 1-2 "Survey Your World" and "Identify Your Most Wanted" (p. 27-50)

Before the Session
1. Before the group session, spend time making a list of the people in your circles of influence. Prepare as complete a list as possible prior to our next session.
2. Begin praying during the week that God will draw these people to faith in Christ.
3. Work through the activities on pages 42-43 to identify your most wanted. Write their names and begin gathering information on each one on the forms on pages 44-48.

During the Session
[Optional for the leader: tell in your own words one or more of the illustrations from *Concentric Circles of Concern* (see *Final Command* (FC) pp. 27, 40, and 50)].
1. Discuss each of the ways listed that God might lead you to identify a person for your most wanted list. In which of these ways did you sense God leading you to identify one (or more) of your most wanted?
2. Divide into small groups (3-5). Ask each person to describe:
    –one of your most wanted
    –how God seemed to lead you to identify this one
    –what your relationship with this person is like
    –how the group can join you in prayer for this person
3. Turn to page 49. Which of these prayer suggestions seem to be most meaningful or practical in praying for your most wanted.
4. In your small group take an extended time praying very specifically for each of the most wanted people mentioned to the group. Also pray for each other that God will use you all to reach your most wanted for faith in Christ.

Action 3: "Reconcile Broken Relationships" (pp. 51-59)

[Because of the depth of this section of material and the time required to complete it, you may want to divide the lesson into two or more parts.]

[Optional for the leader: tell in your own words one or more of the illustrations from *Concentric Circles of Concern* (see FC p. 53)].

1. How did the parable of the PVC pipe speak to you about the importance of relationships in reaching people for Christ?
2. Volunteers: How did you respond to the activity at the bottom of page 53 and why?
3. Volunteers: Share how God has spoken to you about idols of the heart or some sin area in their vertical relationship to God. If appropriate, pray for those who share.
4. Volunteers: share how God has spoken to you about broken relationships you have that need to be made right. What has God already done to guide you to reconcile a broken relationship. Respond in prayer as appropriate (thanksgiving, for a forgiving spirit, strength to reconcile, etc.).
5. Review the lists for the offender and the offended and other teachings on forgiveness (pp. 58-59). Which of these suggestions or insights was most helpful or meaningful to you and why?
6. Divide into smaller groups (3-5 or so). Ask one member to answer this question regarding reconciling relationships: *How can we pray for you?* Listen to the request, and then pray for the person's need. Ask a second person to share and then pray. Continue until you have prayed for each person.

6. Action 4: "Reveal God's Mercy and Love" (pp. 60-69

[Optional for the leader: tell in your own words one or more of the illustrations from *Concentric Circles of Concern* (see FC pp. 63 and 65)].

1. Volunteers, share testimonies of ways other Christian have shown mercy or love to you.
2. Turn to page 64. Describe the way you responded to the activity. Did God use this list to identify a most wanted person or to show you a way you can reveal God's mercy or love to another person at home, at church, or among your most wanted? If so, how?
3. What are some of the ways God is guiding you to show love by meeting needs or build relationship bridges?
4. Close with prayer for each other and those to whom you will be revealing God's mercy and love.

7. Action 5: "Introduce Jesus Christ" (pp. 69-81)

[Optional for the leader: tell in your own words one or more of the illustrations from *Concentric Circles of Concern* (see FC p. 73)].

1. Discuss your responses to the activity on page 69: Why do people need Jesus Christ?
2. Volunteers: Who introduced you to Jesus Christ? How did you come to place your faith in Him? (p. 71)
3. Volunteers: How did you respond to the parable of the water jug? (p. 72)
4. Take a few minutes for conversational prayer. Ask God to prepare you and your fellow Christians with clean lives so that you will make the gospel appealing through your lives. Ask God for boldness in witness.
5. Which of the ways to introduce Jesus Christ appeal most to you and why? Which ones, if any, have you used in the past to introduce people to Jesus? What were the results?
6. Turn to page 76. Do you sense God calling you or your church to reach out to any of the people groups listed or others that you added? If some in your group have a common interest, make plans to get together and pray about the possibilities of an outreach ministry to that group.
7. Share your responses to the activities related to your divine network (pp. 79-81). Are there people in this group setting that God is guiding you to work with in a divine network? If so, make plans to get together to discuss the possibilities and to pray.
8. Has God has given a burden to several people to participate in a specialized team to reach a group of people for Christ (bottom of p. 80)? If so, get these people together to discuss what God is saying and pray about how you will respond.

8. Action 6: "Teach New Believers to Obey" (pp. 82-87)

1. How were you taught to obey Christ's commands? (p. 82)
2. Volunteers only: How are you doing with your obedience? How did you respond to the activity on page 83?
3. Discuss the three ways people may approach Bible study (p. 84) and how you and your church generally approach Bible study. Do you sense that you need to do more to make your Bible study and discipleship Christ centered?
4. List ways your church already helps new believers learn to obey the Lord's commands (p. 85).

5. In what ways can you and your church improve your obedience to the final command by teaching new believers and by growing in your own obedience? (p. 86)
6. What difference do you think you could make as a church if you immediately began helping new believers reach out to the people in their world with the gospel? (see p. 87)
7. Pray that God will guide you and your church to do an effective job of teaching every member to obey the commands of the Lord Jesus.

9. Action 7: "Go to the Ends of the Earth" (pp. 88-97)

1. How much of the world has God assigned to your church for you to be His witnesses? (pp. 88-89)
2. Share and discuss your responses to the activities related to the parable of the talents (pp. 89-93). What do you sense God is saying to you and your church? (p. 93) Would it be words of commendation for faithfulness and obedience or judgment?
3. What should be our compelling motivation for taking the gospel to a lost world? (p. 91, 2 Cor. 5:14-15) Is it motivating you and your church?
4. How many of the members in your church may be in danger of receiving the response given to the "wicked, lazy servant"? If you really love your brothers and sisters in Christ, how will you help them find ways to use their gifts in service of the King? Discuss: Can we really love one another as commanded by Christ, and allow the majority of our church remain in disobedience to the final command?
5. What are some of the ways you will seek to develop a missions awareness? What are some meaningful ways you already have become more aware of God's work around the world?
6. How do you sense God may be calling you to support missions? How is missions support a part of obedience to the final command?
7. Do you have to become a missionary to "go to the ends of the earth"? What are some ways your church helps members become involved in missions? What do you sense God may be calling you or your church to do to become more involved in missions?
8. If you have been involved on the mission field in some meaningful way, share your testimony with your small group.

→ Take time to carefully read through the "Final Command Covenant" below to see if you are willing to enter into this covenant with God and with your brothers and sisters in Christ. If you are willing, we will read and pray this covenant together when everyone is ready.

FINAL COMMAND COVENANT

THAT THE WORLD MAY KNOW
Responsive Reading

Leader: Jesus said, "'Do you not say, "Four months more and then the harvest"? I tell you, open your eyes and look at the fields! They are ripe for harvest'" (John 4:35).

All: Lord, today we open our eyes to look on the lost world. We agree with you—the harvest is ripe.

Leader: Jesus said, "'The harvest is plentiful, but the workers are few. Ask the Lord of the harvest, therefore, to send out workers into his harvest field'" (Luke 10:2).

All: Lord of the Harvest, we ask You to call, equip and send out workers into Your harvest field. We ask You to bring in an abundant harvest.

Leader: Jesus commanded, "'All authority in heaven and on earth has been given to me. Therefore go and make disciples of all nations, baptizing them in the name of the Father and of the Son and of the Holy Spirit, and teaching them to obey everything I have commanded you. And surely I am with you always, to the very end of the age'" (Matt. 28:18-20).

All: Lord, we hear and receive your final command to make disciples of all nations. But we confess before You today: As the Body of Christ, we have failed in our faithfulness and obedience to Your final command.

Leader: God promised, "'If My people who are called by My name will humble themselves, and pray and seek My face, and turn from their wicked ways, then I will hear from heaven, and will forgive their sin and heal their land'" (2 Chron. 7:14).

All: Lord, today we choose to humble ourselves before You and one another. We pray and seek Your face. We repent of our sinful ways. Forgive us, we pray, and heal our land.

Leader: Jesus commanded, "'Go into all the world and preach the good news to all creation'" (Mark 16:15).

All: Lord, we will go and preach the good news to our world.

Leader: "If anyone is in Christ, he is a new creation; the old has gone, the new has come! All this is from God, who reconciled us to himself through Christ and gave us the ministry of reconciliation: that God was reconciling the world to himself in Christ, not counting men's sins against them. And he has committed to us the message of reconciliation. We are therefore Christ's ambassadors, as though God were making his appeal through us. We implore you on Christ's behalf: Be reconciled to God" (2 Cor. 5:17-20).

All: O God, thank You for not counting our sins against us. Thank You for making us new creations. We receive this ministry of reconciliation. We will be Your ambassadors.

Leader: Jesus said, "'As the Father has sent Me, I am sending you'" (John 20:21).

All: Lord Jesus, we accept your commission. We will go.

Leader: Jesus said, "'A new command I give you: Love one another. As I have loved you, so you must love one another. By this all men will know that you are my disciples, if you love one another'" (John 13:34-35).

All: Lord, thank you for loving us. We want to be known as Your disciples. We will love one another in words and in deeds for Your glory.

Leader: Jesus prayed, "'I pray also for those who will believe in me through their message, that all of them may be one, Father, just as you are in me and I am in you. May they also be in us so that the world may believe that you have sent me. I have given them the glory that you gave me, that they may be one as we are one: I in them and you in me. May they be brought to complete unity to let the world know that you sent me'" (John 17:20-23)

All: Lord Jesus, thank You for making possible our union with You and the Father.

All: Father, we join with Jesus in asking that You bring us into complete unity so that the world will know Your Son.

Leader: Jesus promised, "'You will receive power when the Holy Spirit comes on you; and you will be my witnesses in Jerusalem, and in all Judea and Samaria, and to the ends of the earth'" (Acts 1:8).

All: Lord, we pray for the fullness and power of Your Holy Spirit. We bind ourselves together today in a holy covenant of unity to carry the gospel to our home town and to the ends of the earth. Amen.

➡ **If you have entered into this covenant with God and others, as a reminder of this event: describe the occasion and place, sign your name, and write today's date below.**

Occasion: _____

Place: _____

Signature: _____

Date: _____

Discipleship Resources

The following resources developed in part by Claude King have been especially designed for use with small groups. Each resource has a place in helping believers grow and mature in their faith. These may help you and your church more fully to obey the final command by "teaching [believers] to observe all things that I have commanded you" (Matt. 28:20). Here's a brief description and purpose for each.

Final Command Resources

> For the most up-to-date and complete listing of small group discipleship resources by Claude King or to place an order visit the web site at:
> **www.FinalCommand.com**

Come to the Lord's Table: A Sacred Assembly of the Church by Claude King with Meditations by Andrew Murray. Final Command Resources, 2001. This book is a three-week study to help the members of a church prepare themselves to celebrate the Lord's Supper or Communion in a worthy manner. The first week helps members review the meaning of the cross and remember the Lord's death until He comes. Week 2 guides members to examine themselves as preparation to partake in a worthy manner. The lessons after the Lord's Table help Christians focus on the manner of life they should live in light of the sacrifice Jesus made for them. My prayer is that we will return to our first love for Christ.

Final Command Action Manual by Claude King. Final Command Resources. This book is designed to help all Christians in your church work together to obey the final command of the Lord by participating in the process of making disciples. Members will work together to undertake seven actions to lead others to faith in Christ. Leader's material and a variety of use plans are included in this book. This book is especially prepared for introduction in a half day workshop or retreat. It is a natural next step following a use of *Come to the Lord's Table.*

LIFEWAY DISCIPLESHIP RESOURCES

> The following resources are available from
> LifeWay Bookstore 1-800-233-1123
> or online at www.LifeWayStores.com

Concentric Circles of Concern: Seven Stages for Making Disciples by W. Oscar Thompson, Jr., Carolyn Thompson Ritzmann, and Claude V. King. Broadman & Holman Publishers, 1999. This 208-page book is filled with moving relational evangelism testimonies and guides individuals and small groups to understand and apply "Seven Stages for Making Disciples." Chapters include personal and small-group learning activities. Though not required for use with *Final Command*, it provides a valuable resource for explanation and illustration for pastors and small group leaders.

Experiencing God: Knowing and Doing the Will of God (workbook) by Henry T. Blackaby and Claude V. King. LifeWay Press, 1990. This 224-page 12-unit workbook guides individuals into an intimate and personal relationship with God through which they come to know and do His will. Small groups will learn to function as the Body of Christ as they follow God's will together. Leaders will need a copy of the following leader's guide.

Experiencing God Leader's Guide by Claude V. King. LifeWay Press, 1990. This 64-page book provides resources and small group learning activities for a study of *Experiencing God* workbook. A wide variety of other *Experiencing God* resources are available from LifeWay Press.

Experiencing God (Trade Book) by Henry T. Blackaby and Claude V. King, Broadman & Holman Publishers, 1994.

Fresh Encounter: God's Pattern for Revival and Spiritual Awakening by Henry T. Blackaby and Claude V. King. LifeWay Press, 1993. This 96-page workbook leads individuals in a six-week study of God's pattern in Scripture and history for revival and spiritual awakening. It provides a biblical call to repentance and return to the Lord. Fresh Encounter can help individuals and churches return to the Lord and reestablish the foundations necessary for fruitfulness in reaching a lost world. A church is encouraged to study this course all at the same time and in small groups as they seek to experience genuine revival as a church. Leaders will need a copy of the following leader's manual.

Churches will benefit from the additional resources in the leader's kit.

Fresh Encounter Leader's Manual by Henry T. Blackaby and Claude V. King. LifeWay Press, 1993. This 120-page manual provides administrative suggestions for use of all the *Fresh Encounter* resources. It also provides small group learning activities for guiding the six-week study of the workbook described above.

Fresh Encounter Leader's Kit. LifeWay Press, 1993. This kit contains a copy of the workbook and leader's manual described above as well as an introductory video message to *Fresh Encounter* by Henry Blackaby, six 30-minute "plumb line" video messages by Henry Blackaby, a member's book for use with the plumb line messages, and twelve 30-minute audiocassette messages by Henry Blackaby and Avery Willis discussing leadership for times of revival and spiritual awakening.

Fresh Encounter (Trade Book) by Henry T. Blackaby and Claude V. King, Broadman & Holman Publishers, 1996.

In God's Presence: Your Daily Guide to a Meaningful Prayer Life by T. W. Hunt and Claude V. King. LifeWay Press, 1994. This 96-page workbook is designed for a six-week study of prayer. Individuals learn six types of prayer by studying biblical examples and praying in their private devotions five days during the week. The built-in leader's guide helps a group learn to pray together in agreement. The small group meeting becomes a prayer meeting where members practice what they have been learning during the week. The goal of the study is to help churches become houses of prayer.

The Mind of Christ (workbook) by T. W. Hunt and Claude V. King. LifeWay Press, 1994. This 224-page workbook is a 12-week introduction to a lifelong process of becoming like Jesus Christ. Participants study the life and teachings of Christ and spend time in prayer and study as God works to renew their minds into the image of His Son. Small groups help members understand and apply truths to life so that the Body of Christ is pure and reveals Christlikeness to a lost world. Leaders will need a copy of the following leader's guide.

The Mind of Christ Leader's Guide by Claude V. King. LifeWay Press, 1994. This 64-page book provides resources and small group learning activities for a study of *The Mind of Christ* workbook.

The Mind of Christ Leader's Kit. LifeWay Press, 1994. The message of this course can be studied using the workbook above or through audiocassettes or videotapes where T. W. Hunt teaches the message in a conference setting. The kit includes the workbook, leader's guide, audiocassettes, a videotaped conference (6 hours), listening guide, and two one-hour worship videos on the Crucifixion and Resurrection of Christ. This kit is not required for the workbook study.

OTHER DISCIPLESHIP RESOURCES
(available from your local Christian bookstore or Internet bookstore)

Break Down the Walls: Experiencing Biblical Reconciliation and Unity in the Body of Christ by Raleigh Washington, Glen Kehrein, and Claude V. King. Moody Press, 1997. This 210-page workbook provides a 10-unit study of biblical reconciliation and unity. Developed for Promise Keepers, it guides men in a study of related Scriptures and then helps them understand and apply eight principles for reconciliation and unity. Special emphasis is given to unity of the Body of Christ across racial and denominational lines. Built-in leader's materials guide small-group discussions and sharing to develop intentional, sincere, and sensitive relationships with brothers in Christ who are different racially, ethnically, or denominationally.

Interacting with God in Ephesians 1-3 by Gene A. Getz and Claude V. King. Back to the Bible Publishers, 1998. This 146-page workbook is an interactive Bible study of the first half of Ephesians—Paul's letter on what the church is and how it is to function. Each of the 12 lessons includes word studies, learning activities, and guides to help learners interact with God in their private Bible study. Built-in leader's materials help small groups function as the Body of Christ to one another as "minichurches." New members can be added throughout the 12-week study. This tool is valuable not only in developing oneness in the Body of Christ but can also provide an environment for outreach to people in your circles of influence.

Interacting with God in Ephesians 4-6 by Gene A. Getz and Claude V. King. Back to the Bible Publishers, 1999. Same as above for the second half of Ephesians. Since each lesson stands alone, some groups may choose to study this "practical" half of Ephesians first and then turn to the more doctrinal (yet still very practical) emphasis in Ephesians 1-3 above. Either order is appropriate.